Where to

CW01455986

KENT

AN INFORMATIVE GUIDE TO EATING OUT IN KENT

Editor: Alison Moore
Art and Design: Simon Baker, Michelle Power
Compilation: Mervyn Woodward

CONTENTS

Cover Photograph: The Spa Hotel, Mount Ephraim, Tunbridge Wells.

Of Hops and Vines by Mervyn Woodward

Published by Kingsclere Publications Ltd.
Highfield House, 2 Highfield Avenue,
Newbury, Berkshire, RG14 5DS

Produced by the Norman W. Hardy Printing Group, 112 Bermondsey Street, London SE1 3TX, tel: 01 378 1579 at
Avon Litho Ltd, Mason's Road, Stratford-upon-Avon, Warwickshire, CV37 9NF.

Distributed in the UK by AA Publishing,
The Automobile Association,
Fanum House, Basingstoke, Hampshire, RG21 2EA

ISBN 0 86204 152 X

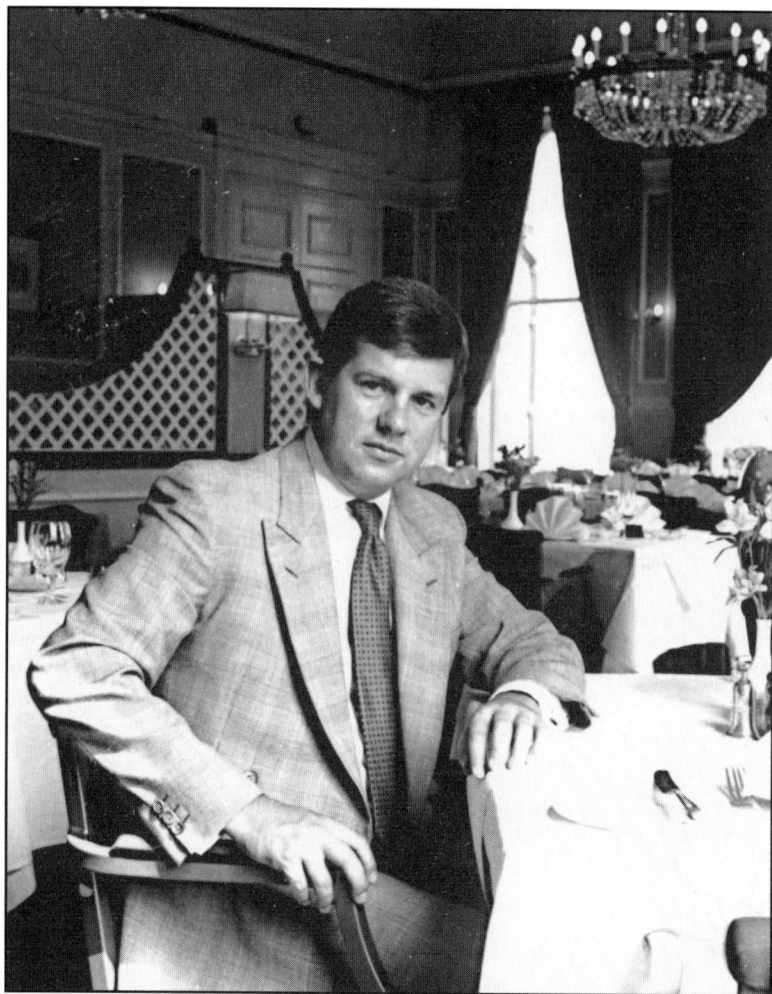

Peter Lowe

Foreword

By Peter Lowe

I graduated from Westminster College in the summer of 1979 and was fortunate to spend the next eight years of my career working in some of London's top hotels. The little free time I had was spent pursuing my hobby of sampling the capital's vast variety of foods and styles of cuisine, as well as tasting some very fine wines.

My appointment as the general manager of The Spa three years ago was therefore my first outside London and, looking back, I remember feeling excited at the prospect of pursuing my hobby further afield. After perusing the pages of the 1987 Where to Eat in Kent guide, I was eager to try out some of the local competition ranging from top class dining to the friendly public house.

One of my first jobs here at The Spa was to alter the menu. Together with our chef and restaurant manager I decided to produce weekly Table d'hôte luncheon and dinner menus for our Chandelier Restaurant. We feel these offer our guests a wide choice of dishes and good value for money, coupled with fine, traditional service for which The Spa is locally renowned.

If you have a similar hobby to mine, I am sure you will find Where to Eat in Kent an invaluable guide, and I would like to hope that one day I may be welcoming you to The Chandelier Restaurant here at The Spa Hotel.

Peter Lowe
General Manager, The Spa Hotel, Mount Ephraim, Tunbridge Wells

Chef's Choice

*In each of our regional **Where to Eat** guides, we ask an experienced chef, well respected in the area, to prepare one of his favourite menus:*

M ike Nixson is head chef at the highly esteemed Chilston Park, Sandway, near Maidstone in Kent. After his first year's study at Guildford, Mike opened his first restaurant for a friend in the airlines, and then resumed his studies. After completing his studies, he went as chef to Elton John's restaurant 'Friends' in Covent Garden. From there he went to the Inn on the Park (London) for two years, and then to the Inn on the Park (Toronto) for a further one and a half years, returning to take a position as chef at London's Hilton International. Finally, after four years in Bermuda, he arrived at Chilston Park.

"When making plans for each day's menu, my policy is, and always has been, to create my selection around the availability of only the freshest of the day's seasonal produce, much of which is produced locally".

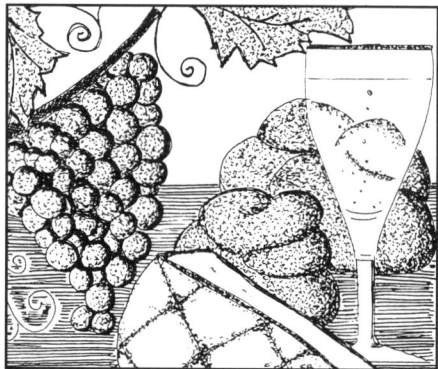

STARTER
Pan-fried fillet of Chilston trout with a tomato and basil cream sauce.

WINE
Chablis premier cru Fourchaume 1988

A glorious trout, fresh from our own lake, with a wonderful use of basil and tomato.

MAIN COURSE
Hot smoked breast of Gressingham duck with cider and apple. Turnips in caramel, timbale of spinach and tomato, pomme cocotte.

WINE
Clos du Clocher Pomarol 1987

Smoked to order, over apple wood. The duck is local and the cider is made in Chilham.

DESSERT
Trio of chocolate mousse with a light coffee-bean sauce.

WINE
Californian or Australian orange muscat

This meal deserves a really sweet, rich dessert, and this is it.

The wines were selected to complement each dish by Chilston Park's Sommelier Graham Powell, who came to Chilston from the Gleneagles Hotel.

OF HOPS AND VINES

Of all the counties in England, none is more famous for the excellence of its produce than Kent, the county that has long been known as the garden of England.

Famous for its hop-gardens, apple orchards, woodland and pastures, the scope extends from farm produce and dairy cattle to Kentish lamb (considered to be the world's best) and the country's finest vineyards.

The Kentish coastal waters provide some of the best seafood available from the famed oysters of Whitstable, which are once again being produced, to Dover sole, plaice and dabs, turbot, monkfish, mussels, squid and, of course, the king of the sea — the herring. As far as fruit is concerned, the Kentish orchards reign supreme. In the Festival of Fruit and Flowers, held at Leeds Castle in mid-September 1989, over 2000 different varieties of apple were displayed, along with over 300 varieties of pear! Many of these came from the national fruit collection at Brogdale, Faversham, where research and development ensures that no varieties of fruit are allowed to die out as a result of intensive marketing of apples and pears that are easier to grow, harvest, store or sell.

Here too, in the county of Kent, you will find the finest wines, both organic and non-organic, from established vineyards such as Lamberhurst Priory and Biddenden, recognised internationally and acclaimed for their excellence. Most of the English wines are white, and range from dry to medium sweet. Rather similar to German Hock or Moselle in style, they have a fresh taste, a cool crisp acidity and a rather fuller flavour than the Continental wines with which they are compared. In fact, many Kent wines are exported to the Continent. Wine making has been carried on in England since Roman times, but is now one of the success stories of agriculture. E.E.C. regulations mean that all English wines have to bear the

words 'table wine' on the label. The English Vineyard Association have, however, introduced a 'seal of quality' so look out for that when buying. Also do NOT confuse 'English' wines with 'British' wines; the former is made from grapes grown here whereas British wines are made from grapes and concentrates imported from Europe — which can mean any part of Europe. Cider is made from local apples in Kent, and this is the county which originated Cherry Brandy, which is made from the Morello cherry. The slightly almond flavour originates from the crushed cherry stones which are added to the pulped fruit.

Cherries, strawberries, raspberries, gooseberries, plums, damsons, loganberries and sweetcorn are also grown, and Romney Marsh potatoes are renowned for their excellent flavour. In September there are still jobs for hop-pickers. This used to be one of the great traditions of the county, when Londoners (in particular) took their annual holiday and came down to Kent by the bus- and trainload for the hop-picking. They lived in hop-huts on the various farms, cooking over wood-fires in the evenings, and they were paid a piece-rate wage which depended upon the quantity of hops gathered. They were paid, originally, in hop-tokens which were usually cast in metal, with a symbol identifying the farm, and having values of one, five, ten, 20 and 50 bushels. The farmer exchanged these for cash each Saturday, and they were also taken in lieu of cash by the local village shops and public houses. Needless to say, the traders and innkeepers did a fine trade during the

hop-picking season. Although the work is now almost entirely mechanised, hop trainers, gatherers, tractor drivers and others are still employed as casual labour during the season, many living in the hop-huts which you can still find throughout Kent.

The hops, when gathered, are dried in the oast houses, scores of which are still operating. Then, when dried, they are gathered into the huge sacks known as 'hop pockets'. The hops are used in beer to give that distinctive flavour, and some of the fine independent breweries in the county, such as Shepherd Neame of Faversham, have been using them for centuries. Oddly enough, the hop was only used in beer and ale after the beginning of the 16th century, before which it was used as a vegetable! Real ales such as Masterbrew, Best Bitter, and the extremely strong Bishop's Finger, are some of Shepherd Neame's delights as well as Keg Abbey and Keg Mild, and their own range of lagers and bottled beers. Honey (still the basic ingredient for making mead) is made from nectar gathered by the bees from the Kentish orchards, and is also used instead of sugar in 'Kent Lent Pie'. In the days when Lent was strictly observed, many cooks became most ingenious at thinking up new dishes to break the monotony of their abstemious diet. This dish, also known as Kentish Pudding Pie is rather like a baked cheesecake, and is originally thought to have been a Folkestone recipe. More of Kent's favourites are the flat oval loaves, indented in the centre, traditional to the county and called Kentish Huffkins. They have a slightly more open texture than ordinary bread, and are considered to be something of a delicacy.

As one might expect, in this great fruit-growing area, fruit is often used in savoury recipes, and a particular favourite of mine is the dish known as 'Kentish Pigeons in a Pot of Plums' a traditional dish of the county. The sharpness of the fruit blends and contrasts deliciously with the pigeons and, combined with onions, cloves, herbs and port becomes a feast fit for an Emperor. One must also give mention of Kent Cobs, or cobnuts, those wonderful large nuts one may gather in late September, not unlike a very large hazelnut (but much tastier). Look out for them in the shops when visiting the county in September and October.

In this beautiful and gentle county you will find inns, hotels and restaurants where every conceivable taste is catered for. The great traditional roasts of Olde England, together with stews with dumplings, casseroles and puddings, pies and flans, go hand in hand with the very best of Italian cooking, French *haute cuisine* and provincial style cookery, as well as Greek, Hungarian, German, Russian and American kitchen magic! A taste of Kent is just that, plus a taste of the Kentish way of preparing the very best produce to create recipes, dishes and specialities from all over the world. Well — what are you waiting for? Hop to it.

Introduction

T his *Where to Eat* guide has been compiled to offer readers a good cross-section of eating places in the area. We do not only concentrate on the most expensive or the 'most highly rated' but endeavour to provide details of establishments which cater for all tastes, styles, budgets and occasions. Readers may discover restaurants (formal and informal), pubs, wine bars, coffee shops and tearooms and we thank proprietors and managers for providing the factual information.

We do not intend to compete with the established 'gourmet guides'. *Where to Eat* gives the facts — opening hours and average prices — combined with a brief description of the establishment. We do not use symbols or ratings. *Where to Eat* simply sets the scene and allows you to make the choice.

We state whether an establishment is open for lunch or dinner and prices quoted are for an à la carte three course meal or a table d'hôte menue, including service, as well as an indication of the lowest priced wine. However, whilst we believe these details are correct, it is suggested that readers check, when making a reservation, that prices and other facts quoted meet their requirements.

Two indexes are included at the back of the guide so that readers can easily pinpoint an establishment or a town or village. We always advise readers to use these indexes as, occasionally, late changes can result in establishments not appearing in a strictly logical sequence.

We hope that *Where to Eat* will provide you with the basis for many intimate dinners, special family occasions, successful business lunches or, perhaps, just an informal snack. A mention of this guide when you book may prove worthwhile. Let us know how things turned out. We are always pleased to hear from readers, be it praise, recommendations or criticism. Mark you envelopes for the attention of 'The Editor, Where to Eat Series'. Our address is:

> Kingsclere Publications Ltd.
> Highfield House, 2 Highfield Avenue,
> Newbury, Berkshire, RG14 5DS.

We look forward to hearing from you. Don't forget, *Where to Eat* guides are now available for nearly every region of Britain, Ireland and the Channel Islands, each freshly researched and revised every year. If you're planning a holiday contact us for the relevant guide. Details are to be found within this book.

Where to Eat

KENT

The Spa Hotel

MOUNT EPHRAIM   TUNBRIDGE WELLS
Tel (0892) 20331 Fax (0892) 510575 Telex 957188 SPATEL

THE SPA HOTEL

Mount Ephraim, Tunbridge Wells. Tel: (0892) 20331. Telex: 957188SPATEL. Fax: 0892 510575.

Hours: *Open for morning coffee, lunch, afternoon tea and dinner (last orders 9.30pm.)*

Average prices: *A la carte from about £22; table d'hôte lunch £15, dinner £19 + 10% service charge.*

Wines: *From about £10 per bottle.*

This incomparable hotel was originally built as a mansion for Sir George Kelly and has been a hotel since 1880. It is often said to be the loveliest hotel in southern England, and the Goring family, who have owned it for many years, are justifiably proud of the fine reputation and high esteem in which The Spa is held. General Manager Peter Lowe, who has kindly written the foreword for this year's edition of 'Where to Eat — Kent' has introduced entirely new menus, giving greater freedom of creativity to his excellent team of chefs who work with the skill and guidance of master chef James Donaldson, the one person who has done so much over many years to contribute to the hotel's fine name. The luncheon menu features starters such as veloute of fish with saffron and scallops, potted kippers with hot buttered toast, deep fried leek turnovers with carrot sauce or marinated seafood in a raspberry vinaigrette. Main courses offer seafood Bercy, pan fried trout with cashew nuts and vegetables, fillet of lemon sole with courgettes, sauté of beef with beer and onions or brochette of mixed meats, fruit pilaff and peppers sauce. Sweets from the trolley. The table d'hote dinner menu has a wider range of selections to tempt the palate, with lamb cutlets reforme competing for your attention with tournedos Café de Paris, picattas of pork Romana and other original and delicious dishes. There is seasonal game of course, excellent fresh fish creations and enough to satisfy the most exacting requirements. The à la carte is, as you would expect, exceptional. Rainbow trout, Dover sole, fillet steaks are included as main courses with prices ranging from £11 up to £30 for a chateaubriand with Bearnaise sauce (for two people) or roast best end of lamb with herbs (again for two) at £26. There are vegetarian dishes, delicious starters and desserts, to be followed by coffee and petits fours. The hotel has fine amenities including a beauty therapy clinic, games room, heated indoor swimming pool, fully equipped gym, a dance studio with daily aerobic classes, floodlit tennis courts, sauna, croquet lawn and an adjacent nine-hole golf course. All major cards welcome. Every facility for conferences, weddings, private parties and functions. Very high degree of luxury & comfort.

THE ROYAL WELLS INN

Mount Ephraim, Tunbridge Wells, Kent, TN4 8BE, (0892) 511188
Fax (0892) 511908

THE ROYAL WELLS INN

Mount Ephraim, Tunbridge Wells. Tel: (0892) 511188. Fax: 0892 511908.

Hours: *Open for lunch and dinner. Bar meals except Sun (last orders 9.45pm).*

Average prices: *A la carte £20 and £27.50; Mon to Sat lunch £10.75; Dinner Mon to Thurs £13.75.*

Wines: *House wines £6.85 & £9.75 per bottle.*

Overlooking the common from its fine position at the top of Mount Ephraim, The Royal Wells Inn is a most impressive and graceful building, with the royal crest mounted upon its roof. The crest honours Queen Victoria who, as a young princess early in the 19th century, made frequent visits to the hotel.

Today it is a traditional and family-run hotel, but Victoria's presence is still strongly felt. The original conservatory restaurant in particular reflects this for it was in Victoria's reign that conservatories first became popular, as decorative sitting rooms for the ladies of the house. Today a multitude of hanging plants and fresh garden colours recapture the atmosphere, and provide an elegant backdrop for the cuisine of Head Chef Robert Sloan. Menus change constantly, and aim to place interesting dishes alongside the more traditional English roasts, casseroles, steaks and fish dishes. Eels in armagnac and a red wine sauce feature, as do Jerusalem artichokes with a Spanish timbale, and both show the original thinking that goes into the planning and creation of the menus. Other typical dishes that might be found on the menu include breast of pheasant with port, fresh oysters, mussels with saffron and goujons of monkfish. For dessert try the ever popular chocolate roulade. There is an extensive wine list to complement the high standard of the cuisine.

For a lighter snack, try Alan's Bar with its pine furnishings and most interesting motoring memorabilia. One of the hotel's most treasured possessions is a 1909 Commer bus once owned by Lord Lonsdale, founder of the A.A.

The luxurious accommodation offers 25 comfortable bedrooms, furnished to the same Victorian theme, all with interesting touches such as brass bedsteads and ruched floral curtains.

The hotel has excellent facilities for conferences, private parties, directors' dining, business meetings, seminars and — naturally — weddings!

Ideally suited for visiting Royal Tunbridge Wells and surrounding places of interest including Penshurst Place, Scotney Castle, Bayham Abbey, Leeds Castle, and Bateman's, Rudyard Kipling's home in Burwash.

SANKEY'S SEAFOOD BAR & RESTAURANT AT THE GATE

Mount Ephraim, Tunbridge Wells. Tel: (0892) 511422.

Hours:	*Open every day except Sat lunch, Sun and Bank Holidays.*
Average prices:	*A la carte £20 (average); bar meals from £4.*
Wines:	*House wine from £7 per bottle. £1.50 per glass.*

There is no better-known seafood restaurant in the county. This is Guy Sankey's third restaurant — each more lovely than the last — and seats over 60 people in auberge-style comfort, in an atmosphere which is both interesting and different. The menus change from day to day, there are different daily specials, and you are always certain to find lobsters, oysters and crabs in abundance! Seafood is bought-in fresh and from different suppliers, and there are also one or two meat and vegetarian dishes for those who so prefer. Start with Cuan Bay rock oysters perhaps, or the Gate's excellent fish soup containing fresh mullet, conger eel and John Dory, served with rouille and gruyere. There are potted shrimps, moules marinière, Dublin Bay prawns — from Scotland(!), stuffed Cornish clams, Queenies (baby scallops — very popular in this part of the world and quite hard to find). There's smoked eel, sweet cured herrings, skate, bass, salmon and Dover sole, crab claws, Greenland prawns, wing of skate, and monkfish — not to mention cod, turbot, halibut and paella. Really the choice is astounding; the dishes and recipes uncomplicated and straightforward — as they should be. First rate. Access and Visa.

SANKEY'S

Seafood Bar and Restaurant
at The Gate

39 Mount Ephraim
Royal Tunbridge Wells
Kent TN4 8AA
(0892) 511422

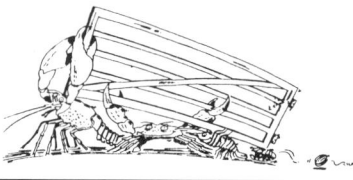

THE BARN

Lonsdale Gardens, Tunbridge Wells. Tel: (0892) 510424.

Hours: *Open for lunch and dinner every day (last orders 10.30pm).*
Average prices: *A la carte £11 to £17; light meals from £2; Sun lunch £6.50.*
Wines: *House wine £5.95 per bottle; wine by the glass £1.20.*

Simon and Nikki Bell took over this delightful restaurant in September 1989. With over twelve years experience in catering and management behind them they have brought a new concept and enthusiasm to this restaurant, and it has become a stylish and popular place to meet for lunch and dinner, and is a most welcome venue in the centre of this really beautiful town. The luncheon menu when Where to Eat visited The Barn offered three starters; home-made soup of the day, melon gondola or prawn cocktail. The choice of a main course had chicken breast filled with prawn and lobster, venison in red wine, sirloin steak or salmon in asparagus sauce. Black Forest gateau, cheese and biscuits or finale ice cream — plus coffee, concluded the meal and this was for the all-inclusive price of £6.95. On the à la carte menu there was a choice of ten starters, nineteen main courses, and desserts of many varieties, fresh each day. Crab bisque, smoked trout, vichyssoise and French onion soup were among the well balanced selection, and main courses included filet be boeuf en croûte, chateaubriand, rack of lamb, filet de porc Normandie, escalope de veau cordon bleu, caneton aux cerises noires, and poussin a'la diable. Booking in advance advisable.

THE BARN

LONSDALE GARDENS, TUNBRIDGE WELLS

THE BROKER'S ARMS

	5 – 11 Langton Road, Tunbridge Wells. Tel: (0892) 541000.
Hours:	*Open for coffee, lunch and dinner. Closed Sun evening dinner, Sat lunchtime. Bar meals available at all times. Full Sun lunch, limited choice of bar meals Sun evening.*
Average prices:	*Fixed price dinner £15; bar meals £3.75; lunch £10.50; Sun Lunch £8.95.*
Wines:	*From £6.50 per bottle.*

Here, in this delightful free house inn and restaurant, you will find traditional English food and real ales. Greene King Abbot from Suffolk, Harvey's Best (Sussex), Marston's Pedigree from Burton-on-Trent, plus one or more guest ales give a well chosen variety to choose from. Food, all prepared in the kitchens of the inn's restaurant, places firm emphasis on fresh locally produced fare, and some five daily specials are featured on the blackboard in addition to the regular menu, so that you have a good choice ranging from fresh fish, steaks and steak sandwiches, garlic mushrooms, chef's pate, moules marinière, ploughman's lunches and others too numerous to detail. Peter and Myra Chipchase are your hosts, and The Broker's Arms is one of the only two free houses in Tunbridge Wells. The restaurant seats 35 and there is a fine functions room where parties and weddings can be catered for up to 40 people. The location of the inn is just opposite the famed Spa Hotel. Visa/Access welcome.

THE BULL

79 Frant Road, Tunbridge Wells. Tel: (0892) 36526.

Hours: *Open for morning coffee, lunch and evening light meals.*

Average prices: *50p to £2.50*

An 18th century coaching inn, The Bull is a genuine unspoilt English pub featuring bar billiards, darts and a skittle alley. Here are sandwiches, beefburgers, cheeseburgers, hot steak pie, toasted sandwiches, filled rolls and similar home-made fare. Cod, plaice, scampi, sausages, hot steak pie and jacket taters at lunchtime; light snacks only in the evening. Tony and Gladys Beer are your appropriately named hosts, and they take great pride in both the quality of the food and in the fine real ales — and beer — that you will find at The Bull.

The Bull

79 Frant Road
Tunbridge Wells
(0892) 36526

THE WEAVER'S RESTAURANT

London Road, Southborough, Tunbridge Wells.
Tel: (0892) 29896.

Hours: *Open for lunch and dinner. Closed Sun eve.*

Wines: *House wine £6.40 per bottle.*

Less than ten minutes from the centre of Tunbridge Wells, The Weaver's Restaurant is full of character and interest. It was originally a farmhouse and still has an impressive Tudor façade. Black and white timbering, high chimney stacks and rows of dormer windows characterise the exterior, whilst, within, the keynote is flexibility. Under the direction of highly-esteemed restaurateur Giuseppe De Bernadi, The Weaver's has built up a sizable reputation. The secret of its success and popularity lies in the fact that Giuseppe believes that the restaurant exists for the benefit of the customer, who can have anything that he or she desires, from caviare and chips to champagne and snails. Menus change regularly, but fresh fish is always a highlight and a house speciality. Dover sole meunière, coquille de fruits de mer Mornay, lobster, crab, oysters and salmon all feature in turn. Specialities include chateaubriand steak and dishes such as escalope de veau Fra Diavolo, beef Stroganoff, steak Diane and a range of poussin (baby chicken) dishes. A comprehensive wine selection accompanies — mainly European, it features some German and Italian vintage. All cards are welcome, and booking in advance is advised.

THE HAND & SCEPTRE HOTEL

21 London Road, Southborough, Tunbridge Wells.
Tel: (0892) 37055. Fax: (0892) 515535.

Hours:	*Open for lunch and dinner every day.*
Average prices:	*A la carte £17.95; table d'hôte £13.50; Sun lunch £9; snacks from £1.95.*
Wines:	*From £6.50 per bottle.*

The Hand & Sceptre dates from 1663 when it was a posting house, providing stabling and accommodation on the main London to Eastbourne Road. With over 350 years of providing a welcome and refreshment for the weary traveller, this fine inn should know a thing or two about making you feel at home and this, together with the reputation for good food, makes The Hand & Sceptre a popular venue for dinner parties, family lunches and directors' dining. The hotel can cater for up to 100 seated or 120 buffet style in catering for delegates or guests. The restaurant seats 60. The food is essentially British traditional in style, with roasts, steaks and fresh garden vegetables together with fresh fish and poultry being the staple selections. Starters such as garlic prawns, deep fried mushrooms and devilled whitebait are followed by fillet steak au poivre, T-bone steaks and similar — try the chicken conchiglie by the way — chicken breasts, pan fried in butter with red and green peppers, garlic, white wine and cream and served with pasta shells. All major cards accepted.

The Hand & Sceptre Hotel
21 London Road, Southborough, Tunbridge Wells. Tel: (0892) 37055

THE KING'S HEAD RESTAURANT

Bessels Green, Sevenoaks. Tel: (0732) 452081 (inn); 740279 (Restaurant).

Hours: *Open for coffee, lunch and dinner. Restaurant closed Sat lunch. Bar meals at lunchtime except Sun.*

Average prices: *A la carte £12.50; Sun lunch £6.*

Wines: *House wine £5.30 per bottle; 95p per glass.*

The colour picture of this lovely traditional English inn-on-the-green was painted by the proprietor, Charles Bowyer, himself. The painting captures both the serenity and the country atmosphere of the inn, which is renowned for its traditional fine fare. The food here offers everything from just a light snack, and a whole range of bar meals, real ales and wine by the glass, to a really first class restaurant menu with over a dozen starters, and as many main course selections. French onion soup, vichysoisse (hot or cold), Greek fish salad, seafood au gratin and gravad lax are just a few examples selected from the list of first courses. Main courses include poached Scottish salmon salad, gigot of lamb with mint butter, pork fillets layered with cream and cheese, fillet or rump steaks, veal cutlets Sevilliana, plus steak and venison pie and many more. Fresh fruit flan, baked honey, almond and apple pudding with cream; and linzertorte (raspberries with almond pastry and cream) are some of the enticements to be found in the dessert menu, and it must be emphasised that all dishes are fresh, home-made. The menu changes every eight weeks.

The Kings Head Restaurant

Bessels Green, Sevenoaks, Kent. Tel: 0732 452081

THE GEORGE & DRAGON

Speldhurst, Kent. Tel: (089 286) 3125/3216.

Hours: *Open every day for lunch and dinner (last orders 10pm).*
Average prices: *A la carte £20; table d'hôte lunch £9, dinner £16.75.*
Wines: *From £6 to £160 per bottle.*

So Much has been written over so many years about this most ancient and historic inn, that it is almost impossible to find new ways to describe The George and Dragon. Perhaps it is not necessary anyway; the inn is a legend; one of the oldest inns in England; haunted, steeped in tales of smuggling, villainy and romance, and enjoying one of the finest reputations for food and wine in the whole of the country. Here, a midst massive oak timbers and antique tables set on huge flagstone floors, you may peruse the Ronay listed 'finest wine list' whilst you contemplate the menus. A whole range of snacks (from £1.50) to the excellent daily specials, there is so much to choose from. Moules marinière, Speldhurst sausage (very famous indeed), sauté lamb's liver with smoked bacon, grilled plaice with prawns — these are just a few of the enticements on the daily luncheon snack menu. Table d'hôte lunch offers five starters and a choice of six or more main courses. Roast Scottish forerib of beef with Yorkshire pudding, or dressed crab with salad — just two examples. The à la carte dinner compares with the finest restaurants and top hotels in the country. Also famed for range of real ales. All major cards.

THE GEORGE & DRAGON
Speldhurst, Kent. Telephone: (089 286) 3125

THE WHITE HART

High Street, Brasted, Westerham. Tel: (0959) 62814.

Hours:	*Open for lunch and dinner. Closed Sun eve during winter.*
Average prices:	*Table d'hôte £5 – £9.50; snacks from £1.50.*
Wines:	*House wine £4.95 per bottle. Good selection from £5.*

This lovely old inn, which dates from the 14th century, has of course become a legend, for it was from here that the young pilots — 'the few' — left to return to their duties at Biggin Hill after an evening's relief from stress at the inn. They were brave days of hardship and courage, and food was rationed. How different all that is 50 years on. The winter months offer delicious roasts and stews, casseroles and pies to enjoy by blazing log fires in warmth and comfort. There are specialities such as moules marinière, veal, salmon, game, fresh fish and shellfish. There are wonderful salads in summer, and, most delightful of all, you can eat out in one of the finest gardens in the south, where the show of petunias in June, July and early August draws enthusiasts from far and wide. The inn has limited bed and breakfast accommodation, and of course is ideally placed for trips to Winston Churchill's home at Chartwell, Quebec House, General Wolfe's family home, and surrounding castles and places of interest. Good bar meals too, with sandwiches, ploughman's, and other fare.

The White Hart

Brasted, Westerham, Kent. Tel: 62814

THE HENGIST

7/9 High Street, Aylesford, Nr. Maidstone. Tel: (0622) 719273. Fax: 0622 715027.

Hours: *Open for lunch and dinner (last orders 9.30pm).*

Average prices: *A la carte £24 (3 course).*

Wines: *House wine £7.90 per bottle.*

This incomparable restaurant is long established and has a reputation county-wide for good food. Owner David Loader named the restaurant after the first Saxon king of Kent, who fought famous battles at Aylesford in 455AD. The continual work of restoration which has created this restaurant now includes a conservatory of the first floor terrace, two exquisite *en suite* bedrooms — so lovely they must be seen to be appreciated — as well as further improvements to the restaurant itself. The menu is changed every week, using only fresh and seasonal produce, and there are many unusual and interesting dishes that set The Hengist apart from other restaurants in this part of the county. Also, in addition to being included in major food guides, The Hengist has won the Clean Food Award for two consecutive years. Try the fillet of brill with lobster and sherry sauce, or the fabulous veal and asparagus pie with its creamy cheese sauce and fluffy pastry crust — just two of a selection of many enticements that are both different and delicious. There is something for every taste on the menus, and all major credit cards are welcome.

"A corner of the conservatory for pre-dinner drinks."

THE HENGIST

7/9 High Street,
Aylesford,
Near Maidstone.
Tel (0622) 719273
Fax (0622) 715027

THE SHANT HOTEL AND PRINCE OF WALES

East Sutton, Nr. Maidstone, Kent. Tel: (0622) 842235.

Hours:	*Open for lunch and dinner (last orders 10.30pm).*
Average prices:	*Meals from £3.95.*
Wines:	*House wine £5.50 per bottle.*

'Where to Eat — Kent' is proud to be able to feature again The Shant Hotel and Prince of Wales. Here, standards are not just maintained — and they have never been less than excellent — they are improved each year, to add new dimensions, facilities, ideas and comforts. In the late spring of this year 1990, the new restaurant opens, with a quality of food and service comparable with the top restaurants in the county. The hotel has facilities for every type of function, and is particularly suitable for private parties, business lunches and dinners, seminars, conferences and directors' dining, in addition to being well established as one of the most attractive places for that 'get together' with a few friends — or a tête-à-tête with someone close. The Prince of Wales — which is an inn within the hotel — caters for light lunches and dinner and offers everything from a simple ploughman's lunch or sandwich to curries, pastas, casseroles and daily specials. Eleven bedrooms, all *en suite*, have every comfort such as colour T.V., tea/coffee making facilities etc. All major credit cards are welcome. The Shant is set in the heart of rural Kent, and is convenient for all attractions.

THE SHANT HOTEL AND **PRINCE OF WALES**
EAST SUTTON, Nr. MAIDSTONE

0622 842235

25

THE FOX & HOUNDS

Wrotham Road, Meopham, Nr Gravesend. Tel: (0474) 812154.
Hours: *Open for lunch and dinner every day (last orders 9.30pm).*
Average prices: *A la carte £13; Sun lunch £5.95; bar meals £1.30 to £4.95.*
Wines: *House wine from £5.50 per bottle.*

This most attractive inn with its 45 seat restaurant is one of the fine Thorley
Tavern establishments, and in 1988 was the winner of the Pub Caterer of the Year
award; runner-up, also, in the publican of the year award! Other accolades have
been given to this prestigious inn including that of being second in the quality
pub of the year competition and also reaching the finals of the licensed trades
award for the best garden. Hosts Guy and Rena Davies are meticulous in
planning their menus, and only fresh local produce is used wherever possible.
Bar meals offer a superb home-made steak & kidney pie, honey-roast ham,
scampi and chicken in the basket, and a whole host of other appetising meals
ranging from sandwiches and ploughman's lunches to filled jacket potatoes and
vegetarian dishes. There is also a special children's menu. The à la carte is
wide in choice. Whitebait, smoked mackerel, Mediterranean prawns and Italian
pasta feature among the starters, and main courses include 16oz T-bone steaks,
mixed grill, escalope of veal, Dover sole, rainbow trout, monkfish in white wine
sauce and — a favourite — Fox & Hounds spare-ribs. Some good vegetarian dishes
too, of which the artichoke heart with cheese sauce is worth special mention. All
four major credit cards are welcome. Real ales; large car park, fine garden.

The FOX & HOUNDS
A THORLEY TAVERN

Wrotham Road, Meopham, Kent.
Telephone: (0474) 812154

THE GREAT DANES HOTEL

Hollingbourne, Nr. Maidstone. Tel: (0622) 30022.

Hours: *Open for lunch and dinner every day.*

Average prices: *A la carte £15; table d'hôte £11.55; dinner £12.75.*

Wines: *House wine £7.50 per bottle. Wide selection.*

One of the most highly esteemed hotels in the south-east, The Great Danes is something of a tradition in Kent, like hops and orchards! Long established, ideally situated and with an enviable reputation for international cuisine, the hotel has 126 fully *en suite* bedrooms, and one of the finest ballrooms and banquetting suites in the county. The Garden Cafe within the hotel is open from 11am to 11pm and has an extensive and reasonably priced menu offering everything from sandwiches and the Great Danes Club Special to starters and main courses with steaks, scampi salad platters, grilled gammon steaks, beefburgers and curry. The evening and weekend menu gives a wider selection, and includes chicken Kiev, grilled plaice, breast of chicken as well as other dishes. There is a vegetarian choice at all times. There is a pool-side menu too, which is most sensible and original. Here are asparagus quiche, pineapple and cottage-cheese filled jacket potatoes and vegetarian specials. Good afternoon tea menu also. Fine conference facilities, banquetting menus, exhibition, and wedding facilities, plus a very special 'daymeet conference package.'

The Great Danes Hotel
Hollingbourne, Maidstone
Tel: (0622) 30022

THE BULL INN

The Hill, Linton, Maidstone. Tel: (0622) 743612.
Hours: *Open for lunch and dinner. Restaurant closed Mon/Tues.*
Average prices: *A la carte £5.50 – £12.50.*
Wines: *£5 per bottle; £1.10 per glass.*

This excellent inn, full of character, serves food to rival the best of restaurants, and you are well advised to book in advance — it is essential at weekends. It is a truly lovely inn, and the views from the large car park at the back of the inn are spectacular, with a panorama of Kent stretching out beneath your feet like a map of the garden of England! There is a beautiful garden too; more like a true country house garden than that you might expect at an inn. The great speciality of The Bull is the superb seafood in which the landlord, David Brown, takes great pride. Starters such as whitebait, fresh sardines, smoked Scottish salmon, smoked eel and prawns in garlic are temptations indeed. The main course offers lobster salad, John Dory, sea bass, Scottish steaks, brill, Dover sole, fresh crab and turbot with a subtle tomato and mushroom sauce. Although seafood is the great speciality, there are also rump, fillet and sirloin steaks, pies, casseroles and an excellent range of bar meals with daily lunch specials. real ales are on draught; there are log fires, old oak beams — the delightful intimate restaurant was once the posting house — and one of the friendliest receptions you'll find in the country. Access/Visa welcome.

THE BULL INN
THE HILL, LINTON
(0622) 743612

THE DOG AND BEAR HOTEL

The Square, Lenham, Nr. Maidstone. Tel: (0622) 858219.

Hours:	*Full hotel hours. Open every day for lunch and dinner.*
Average prices:	*A la carte £15; luncheon £11 – £12; Sun lunch £6.75; snacks and bar meals from £1.25 to £3.50.*
Wines:	*From £6 per bottle.*

This delightful old coaching inn dates from 1602 and is one of Shepherd Neame's superb Invicta country inns. Queen Anne visited the inn in 1704 and the royal coat of arms is displayed above the main entrance. Although the hotel may look much as it did all those years ago, it is now refurbished to the highest standards and has 25 lovely bedrooms, all *en suite*, with colour T.V., direct dial phones, trouser press and shoe polishers. The hotel offers a 'same-day' laundry service. The food is traditional English fare, featuring roasts, grills, fresh fish and game in season. The restaurant, which seats 50, gives a wide selection on the à la carte menu, with starters to appeal to all tastes — over nine to choose from — and main course selections give some unusual and imaginative dishes as well as steaks, mixed grills, crown lamb chops, game pie and grilled lemon sole. The wide selection is also carried through into desserts, with 11 to whet the appetite plus cheeseboard, coffee and liqueurs. Access, Visa and American Express are welcome, and the hotel has fine conference facilities for up to 60 (seated) or 100 (buffet style). The Dog & Bear is included in the major food guides and is R.A.C. and A.A. recommended. Good bar snacks too.

THE SQUARE, LENHAM, MAIDSTONE. (0622) 858219

WHO'D A THOUGHT IT

Grafty Green, Nr. Lenham. Tel: (0622) 858951.

Hours: Open for lunch and dinner (last orders 9.30pm). Restaurant closed Tuesday.

Average prices: A la carte £11.50; snacks from £1.50.

Wines: House wine £4.50 per bottle; 95p per glass.

What a lovely country setting in which to take a weekend break or a holiday. Here, in the heart of the garden of England, in a quaint village is an inn of character, a free house, with ten modern, well-equipped, self-contained double rooms, all with telephones and televisions, and a restaurant with an excellent reputation. Everything from ploughman's lunches and toasted sandwiches, smoked mackerel and salads to T-bone, fillet and gammon steaks, home made pies and curries are available in the inn, and a blackboard features daily specials with a delightful variation including veal, chicken and fresh fish dishes as well as some delectable home made pies. The care and attention to detail of the proprietors, Fred and Joan Mallett, is reflected in every aspect of the inn. A hint of applewood log smoke and the scent of wax-polished oak furniture are the visitor's first welcome. The inn also caters for private parties and 'away from it all' weekends.

GRAFTY GREEN, LENHAM. Tel: (0622) 858951

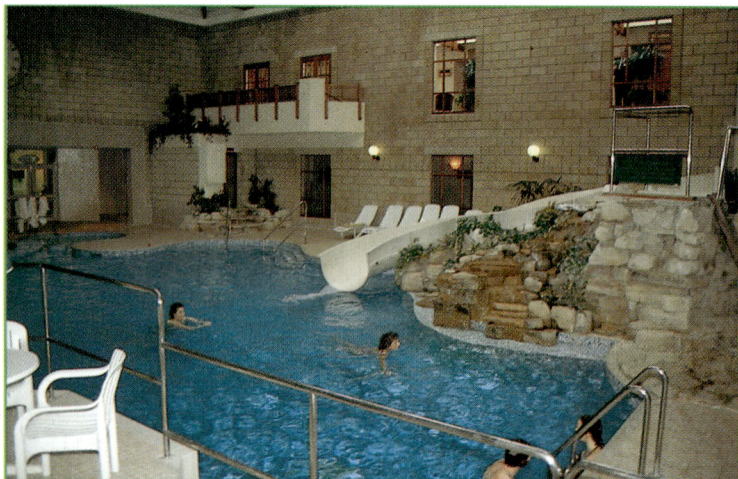

TUDOR PARK HOTEL, GOLF AND COUNTRY CLUB

Ashford Road, Bearsted, Maidstone, Kent. Tel: (0622) 34334.
Telex: 966655. Fax: (0622) 35360.

Hours:	*Full hotel hours. Open for morning coffee, lunch and dinner every day of the week. Afternoon tea is served in the Waterside Grill.*
Average prices:	*A la carte from £19; bar snacks from £1.50.*
Wines:	*Wide selection from £5.95 per bottle.*

The Tudor Park Hotel, Golf and Country Club is one of the superb Country Club Hotels group. Set in its own spacious landscaped grounds, the Tudor Park has its own 18 hole golf course. There are 120 luxurious, fully equipped bedrooms, all *en suite*, with remote control televisions, direct dial telephones, shoe polishers, sky satellite etc, and the hotel can provide full conference facilities for up to 400 delegates, plus banquetting. In all, the grounds and golf course extend to 156 acres.

The Garden Restaurant, under the direction of executive chef Neil Coomber and *Maitre d'hôtel* Aksas Alouani (formerly of the Waldorf), is of international standard, and has been acclaimed for both quality and breadth of imaginative choice, utilising the very best of British traditional fare together with Continental influence and produce. The à la carte offers soups, fish and starters which include Tudor style seafood tagliatelli, terrine of broccoli and carrot, mussel bisque, Icelandic scallops and lobster thermidor. From the entrees and grills you may select from a choice of twelve dishes as varied as noisettes of lamb dijonaise, calves' liver Lorraine, breast of pheasant Stockbury, escalope of veal, supreme of chicken reisling or roast wild duck. There are steaks and veal cutlets, and all are served with fresh vegetables or mixed green salad with choice of dressing. Sorbets and dessert selection from the Butler's Tray, a fine cheeseboard and ground coffee with confectionery conclude the meal. A very well chosen wine list complements the meal, with a good mid-range option.

The hotel is in an ideal location for visitors to the area, and there are many attractions such as Leeds Castle (claimed as the world's most beautiful), the famed Headcorn parachute club, London Flight Centre at Headcorn which operates a sightseeing flight over Leeds Castle as well as full flying training, gliding from Charing, riding and many other sports and attractions for all ages. All major credit cards are welcome. There is a children's menu and full menu room service from 10am to 11pm. Vegetarian meals are available.

THE SHIP INN & SMUGGLER'S RESTAURANT

Teynham, Nr. Sittingbourne. Tel: (0795) 521404.

Hours:	*Open for coffee, lunch and dinner every day of the week.*
Average prices:	*A la carte from £8.50; bar meals from £2.*
Wines:	*From £5.65 per bottle.*

David Pleshnell, editor of Food & Drink Magazine, wrote thus of The Ship Inn and Smuggler's Restaurant, when he visited it in June 1988:

'In truth, I have had but a handful of memorable visits to table in twenty years of following the dubious profession of eating for a living. On the day of my visit to The Ship, I had one of the most memorable meals of my life.'' And there is much much more to the Ship than just the superb food. Over 100 whiskies are kept in stock; there are some 65 single malts alone, and the wine list, international, is one of the most extensive in the south. There are over 80 liqueurs, and The Ship has recently won the Stowell's 'Wine Pub of the Year' award. Landlord Alec Heard is a character indeed. Bearded, jovial and extrovert, he appears in the pages of his menu in varied garb — as a pirate, a Nazi officer and others. He and Lindsay his wife run one of the quaintest and most fascinating inns in the entire country. To try to describe the variety and quality of the food would need a whole chapter! Everything home-made; freshness is all. Fondues with hot crispy French bread — seafood — lobsters, shellfish, Kent lamb — everything for almost every taste. Wonderful.

Telephone Teynham (0795) 521404 and we will direct you here

CHILSTON PARK

Sandway
Lenham
Maidstone
Tel: (0622) 859803

CHILSTON PARK COUNTRY HOUSE HOTEL

Sandway, Lenham, Nr. Maidstone. Tel: (0622) 859803. Fax: 0622 858588. Telex: 966154CHILP.

Hours:	*Open for morning coffee, lunch, tea and dinner.*
Average prices:	*Lunch £16.50, dinner £29.50; Sun lunch £17.50; tea £8.*
Wines:	*House wine from £11 per bottle.*

Judith and Martin Miller have created a whole new meaning to the phrase 'country house hotel'. The restoration and renovation of this magnificent country mansion is unique. As they say in their own newspaper *The Times of Chilston,* 'As with all old and precious things, the care and attention lavished on them is rewarding, but also never ending. With Chilston, the problem is magnified because it has always been a home rather than an hotel. People live at Chilston, albeit for a short time, rather than merely stay, and because of this subtle difference, the whole place exudes a homeliness that has to be maintained.' The charm of Chilston is that, as you step through the front door, you step back in time. You are welcomed into the hall by staff in traditional Edwardian dress. Surrounded by antiques and immense gracious comfort, there is an immediate feeling of well-being, a kind of *déjà vu* — perhaps a part of our heritage? The great log fire which is kept burning all year; the polished riding boots; ancient armour, tapestries; the smell of old oak; polish and peacefulness — here is an oasis of elegance. The butler will lead you through to dine in one of the individually styled dining rooms. There is the red dining room which overlooks the lake and the north downs; the blue dining room with its magnificent chandelier; the cosy private dining room, and the Douglas room for smaller private parties. The book-lined library looking out over the garden is also used for dining. After the meal, the cheeseboard and fresh fruit are served in the drawing room with coffee and liqueurs. Here, diners can luxuriate in the relaxing candlelit atmosphere in front of the log fires or play parlour games and charades. The food at Chilston is also part of the creation of authenticity; traditional fine English fare, using fresh vegetables and fruit from its own gardens, together with wild Scottish salmon, sirloins of Scottish beef, Kentish roast lamb, English spring chicken and seasonal game; sautéd breast of grouse with onion marmalade and soubise sauce; fillet of Dover sole with sorrel and champagne sauce, roast rack of lamb, carved at your table and served with natural gravy and sauce paloise. These are just a few examples from the choice dinner menu. Truly an outstanding experience, Chilston shows what can be done with original thought and real imagination. It is owned and run by Martin and Judith Miller, publishers of Miller's Antiques Price Guide. All major cards welcome.

THE DERING ARMS

Pluckley. Tel: (023 384) 371.

Hours:	*Open for lunch and dinner (last orders 10pm).*
Average prices:	*A la carte £9.50; Sun lunch £12; snacks from £1.*
Wines:	*House wine £5.45 per bottle; £1.10 per glass.*

Once the lodge of the Dering family, the imposing Dering Arms features massive flagstone floors, huge fireplaces and arched doorways. Although the facilities for comfort have been brought up to modern standards, nothing of the character of the place has been lost and the beautiful restaurant is still an aristocratic dining room. The speciality here is fresh fish and seafood, purchased from the coast each day and marked up on the blackboard. There is usually sea bass, bream, salmon, crab, lobster, squid and, occasionally, turbot. The inn is particularly well-known for the seafood special which contains just about everything, whilst, for an alternative to the seafood dishes, there is fillet steak with tarragon and cream, and local trout with lemon and almonds. Owner Jim Buss has, with the help of his chef, won major awards for culinary excellence, and the desserts, such as chestnut and chocolate slice with Cointreau and a cream sauce, exemplify this. A wide choice of wines accompanies the menu. The special gourmet evenings are always popular and it is advisable to book in advance.

THE KING'S HEAD

Church Street, Wye. Tel: (0233) 812418.

Hours: *Open every day for lunch and dinner.*
Average prices: *A la carte £12 to £17; Sun lunch £6.90; bar meals from £2.*
Wines: *From £5.95 to £14.50 per bottle.*

Linda and George Edwards took over this fine inn in 1989 and have made a
complete transformation here. Once again this lovely market-town hotel is
bustling with activity and life, and without doubt this has been very largely
because of the fine food which is served here. Everything is home-cooked,
all the vegetables — with the exception of garden peas — are fresh, and the
menu offers wide choice and top quality. Even the bar meals are all home-
cooked, featuring steak and kidney pie, cottage pie, chicken and ham pie
and some very good vegetarian recipes such as nut and mushroom lasagne.
The hotel has nine bedrooms, seven of which are *en suite*, and all have
colour T.V., tea/coffee making equipment and telephones. At £39 for a
double room or £23.50 single this is considered to be outstanding value for
money, and the hotel also offers special weekend rates. There is a 'senior
citizen' luncheon special every Thursday with a full three course lunch for
just £2.95 which has proved to be most popular. The à la carte offers
starters such as garlic mushrooms, melon and port and escargots in the
evenings, and main courses such as fresh lobster, honey-roast duckling,
venison in red wine, halibut steaks and many others. Access/Visa welcome.

THE KING'S HEAD Church St., Wye, Kent (0233) 812418

BUXFORD MILL

	Bucksford Lane, Great Chart, Ashford. Tel: (0233) 636247.
Hours:	*Open for dinner Tues to Sat. Open for lunch Wed to Sun.*
Average prices:	*A la carte £25; table d'hôte £15.95.*
Wines:	*From £6 (house wine) to £70 per bottle.*

In one of the most exquisite settings in Kent, five minutes from the middle of Ashford, stands Kent's newest restaurant, Buxford Mill. New it may be, but is has been opened by Anita and Barry Law, who have brought their talents as highly esteemed restaurateurs with very many years experience to Ashford. It is Anita Law F.B.I.I. who plans and creates the menus and selects the wines. The decor is quite lovely and in perfect keeping with the atmosphere of this old mill with its spacious comfort and rural setting. Looking first at the table d'hôte menu, you will find such starters as melon & sorbet surprise, followed by rosette of beef fillet with a special red wine sauce; chef's dessert of the day and coffee & *petits fours*. The à la carte menu has such starters as marinated breast of pigeon with asparagus and watercress salad, whole quail or steamed scallops with chive and carrot and a white wine sauce. Main courses give a fine varied selection ranging from tournedos of beef with caramelised shallots, smoked bacon and savoy cabbage served in a claret sauce, magret of duck, or loin of English lamb with fresh thyme and tomato coulis. Wines to complement the menu. Book in advance. All major credit cards accepted.

THE QUEEN'S ARMS

Egerton Forstal, Ashford, Kent. Tel: (0233) 76386.

Hours: *Open for morning coffee, lunch and dinner.*

Average prices: *From £1.50 to £10; Sunday lunch £5 (or less).*

Wines: *From £4.75 per bottle.*

In the very heart of rural Kent, you will find this delightful family-run free house. Off the beaten track but very well worth every effort to find, the Queen's Arms is a perfect example of how an English country inn should look — and should be run. Valerie and Dexter Hogben take enormous pride in their superb home-cooking, and their enthusiasm is reflected in every aspect of this clean and sparkling inn. Only fresh prawns are used in their prawn cocktail; all the soup is home-made, and the season's fresh produce is always used with nothing frozen — ever. The Sunday roast is served with six fresh vegetables — and horseradish from the fields instead of from a jar. There are four real ales; Harveys, Adnams, Tetleys and Bombardier. The last is particularly interesting because that legend of boxing, Bombardier Billy Wells was Valerie's father! Try the super home-made chicken, ham and leek pie, or the lovely tuna quiche — which incidentally is made without eggs. There is a daily special which is featured on the blackboard, and the *pièce de résistance*, if one can say there is one among this selection of fine British fare, is the roast beef — always an H-bone or topside and Yorkshire pudding. Small wonder that this inn is in the major food guides. No credit cards.

THE QUEENS ARMS
Egerton Forstal, Ashford. Tel: (0233) 76386

THE POST HOUSE HOTEL

Canterbury Road, Ashford.
Tel: (0233) 625790. Fax: (0233) 643176.

Hours:	*Open for morning coffee, lunch and dinner.*
Average prices:	*Table d'hôte £14.95; A la carte from £15; bar snacks from £1.75.*
Wines:	*From £6.95 per bottle.*

Post House Hotels are an established way of life for the discerning businessman, and for all those who enjoy the better things in life, but who expect value for money. The Shires restaurant in Ashford's Post House Hotel is both elegant and sophisticated, and yet it is sufficiently informal for one to feel relaxed and at ease when dining with co-directors — or with the whole family on holiday. The menus change daily and with the seasons, and the set price luncheon menu offers, for example, a choice of three starters (Northumberland broth, smoked sea trout or chicken liver terrine) and four main courses (shepherd's pie, whole grilled plaice, roast sirloin of beef or cold cuts from the larder). The evening à la carte can feature English calves' liver, roast rack of lamb, Dover sole, whole young chicken, prime English steak, salmon steak and a vegetable and fresh herb pie. A special 'Shire's Grill' and a seafood grill may also be on the menu. The hotel has 60 bedrooms, all *en suite*, and all have colour television, direct dial phones, mini-bar etc. There are six meeting rooms and full conference facilities.

THE POST HOUSE HOTEL
CANTERBURY ROAD, ASHFORD.
ASHFORD 625790

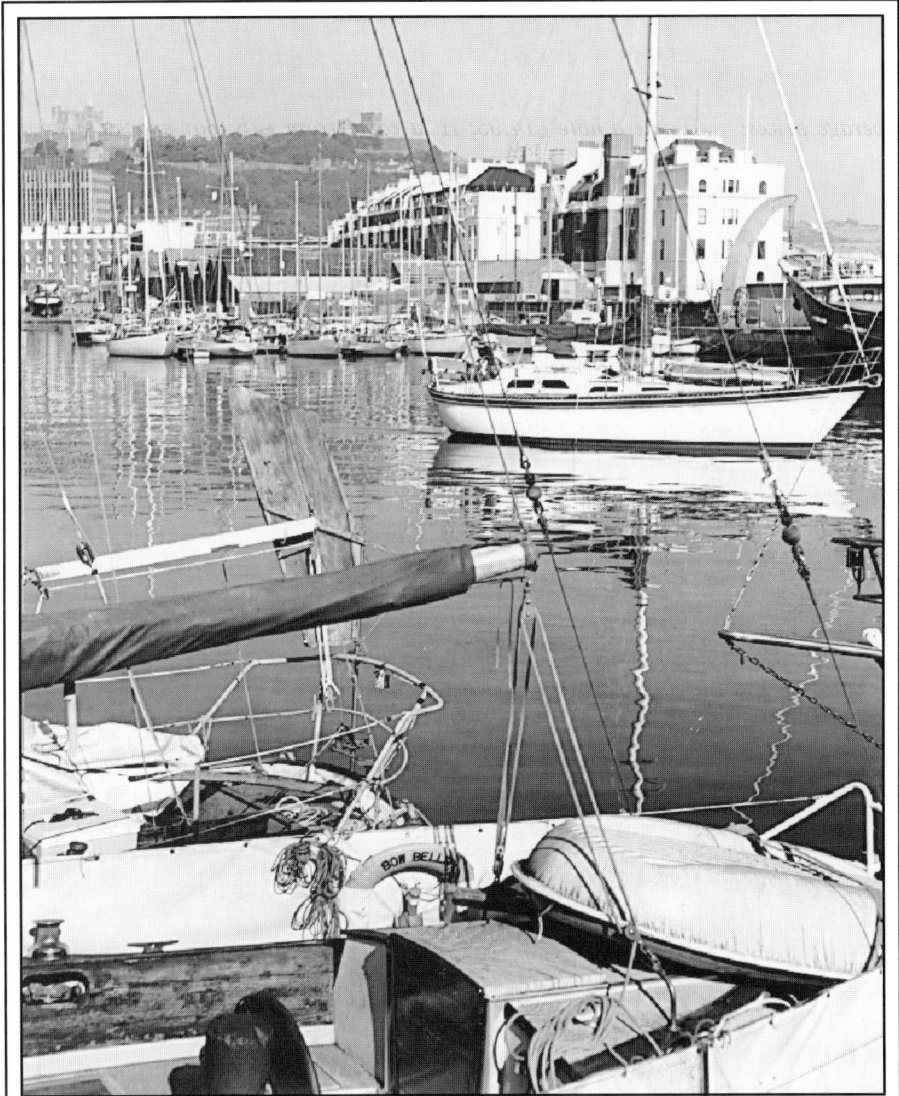

Lovely Kentish boating weather
(Photo courtesy of the Dover Tourist Board)

EASTWELL MANOR
Eastwell Park, Boughton, Aluph, Ashford.
Tel: (0233) 635751. Telex: 966281. Fax: (0233) 635530

EASTWELL MANOR

Eastwell Park, Boughton Aluph, Ashford. Tel: (0233) 635751. Telex: 966281. Fax: 0233 635530.

Hours:	*Open for lunch and dinner.*
Average prices:	*A la carte £30; set lunch £10.50 & £13.50; dinner £25*
Wines:	*House wine from £12.75 per bottle. One of the finest selections in the country.*

This magnificent and elegant country hotel is numbered among the world's finest and has a reputation of international acclaim. Standing in its own parkland of over 60 acres, in the midst of a 3,000 acre estate, it was here, at Eastwell Manor that a Queen of Rumania was born, and both Queen Victoria and Edward VII were frequent guests. The hotel has 23 superbly luxurious bedrooms, each of individual design, all fully *en suite* and equipped with every modern comfort. The lounges, billiards room and bar are graced with huge open fireplaces with stone mantels, carved panelling, leather chesterfield sofas and fine antique furniture.

Eastwell Manor has full conference facilities for up to 50 delegates, and this, combined with the seclusion of the Manor, makes it an ideal venue for boardroom meetings requiring security and seclusion. The hotel has facilities for tennis and croquet, and other leisure pursuits such as golf, shooting, squash, riding and trout-fishing can be arranged locally.

The beautiful wood-panelled dining room is a restaurant which is open to non-residents, and has earned top accolades from the major food guides, and it was here that many of the country's top chefs trained — and in some cases went on to found their own famed restaurants! The very best of English — or more correctly — British fare is the speciality, with game in season, Scottish wild salmon, venison, the roast beef of Olde England, Kentish lamb and fresh river trout being featured on the constantly changing menu as the seasons dictate. To give some examples from the table d'hôte menu, one might, as a starter, choose chilled leek and potato soup with garden chives, or creamed wood mushrooms flavoured with madeira and served in a puff pastry case, or, perhaps, a melon, mango and ginger salad. You might, for main course, choose roast breast of chicken with a herb mayonnaise served on a summer salad, or fillet of Scottish salmon in a light cream sorrel sauce or roast lamb with courgette and tomato timbale. English cheeses with freshly baked walnut and raisin bread follow, as does a choice of hot almond pithiviers with a *compote* of English fruits, or white/dark chocolate ice cream with hazelnut biscuits. You must, from this, be able to imagine the variety and quality of the full à la carte, and it must be mentioned that the extent of the wine cellar is thought to be unequalled within the county — or beyond.

Eastwell Manor is just 30 minutes from the European ferry ports of Dover and Folkestone, and just an hour and a half from London. All major credit cards are welcome.

THE ROYAL OAK

60 Island Road, Upstreet, Nr. Canterbury.
Tel: (0227) 86314.

Hours: *Open for morning coffee, lunch and dinner every day.*
Average prices: *A la carte from £7.50 to £12; bar meals from £1 to £6.50.*
Wines: *From £5 to £12 per bottle.*

'Why on Earth didn't we discover this place before?' is the question you are
most likely to ask yourself after you find The Royal Oak at Upstreet. There
is no simple answer except perhaps that Upstreet is a village you might
tend to drive through in a hurry to be somewhere else. Next time — stop
here. Keith Thomas, Member of the British Institute of Innkeepers, runs a
very fine inn indeed, and the inn offers accommodation with *en suite*
bedrooms, colour televisions, tea/coffee making facilities — the lot! There
are views clear to Dover and Canterbury from the garden at the back of this
inn, and there is an outdoor barbecue here too in summer. The food is first-
rate. Bar meals offer club sandwiches, home-made soup, toasted sandwiches,
chilli con carne, steaks, jumbo sausages with baked potatoes, cheese and
salad and a grand choice of other good food. The restaurant proper gives
excellent value and has favourites such as steak Diane, steak au poivre,
tournedos Rossini, half roast chicken, gammon & pineapple, trout Bretonne
— plus a daily chef's special which has the reputation of being very special
indeed. This is one you must find.

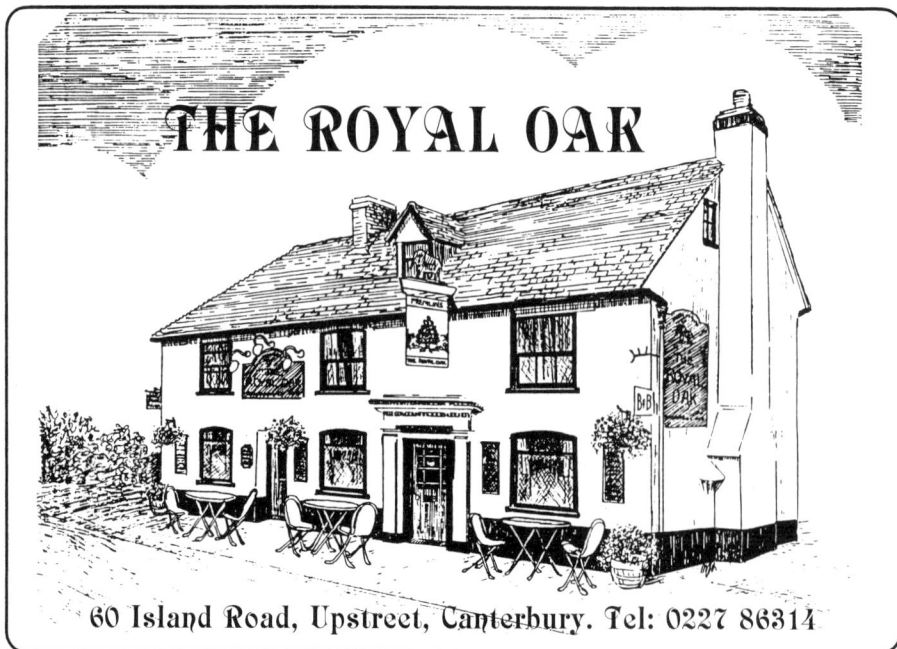

60 Island Road, Upstreet, Canterbury. Tel: 0227 86314

RISTORANTE TUO E MIO

16 The Borough, Canterbury. Tel: (0227) 61471.

Hours:	*Open for lunch and dinner (last orders 10.45pm, 10pm Sun). Closed Mon/Tues lunch.*
Average prices:	*A la carte £13−£17; Sun lunch £8; lunch £8.*
Wines:	*House wine £5.50 per bottle.*

Sample the *dolce vita* at this well-patronised Italian restaurant which has everything and, above all, flair. Close to the Cathedral, it appeals to all the senses — with its snow-white napery, sparkling crystal and gleaming cutlery, it is airy and elegant. The menu is extensive and appetising; the produce is fresh and of the highest quality. Take a seat at a table adorned by a single carnation in a crystal vase and study the menu. Daily specials are seasonally altered, and suggest some interesting varieties. These include partridge or pheasant, sea bass or lobster, moules marinière or scallops, and pasta made freshly on the premises. The menu is too extensive to be able to give any real idea of the choice; suffice it to say that it extends from fried artichoke hearts to fresh grilled sardines, from squid to calves' liver, from veal scallopina to fillet or entrecote steaks. Homely Italian cooking, well-presented; fine Italian wines (over 30 to choose from) and enticing desserts conclude. All major credit cards are welcome and booking is essential.

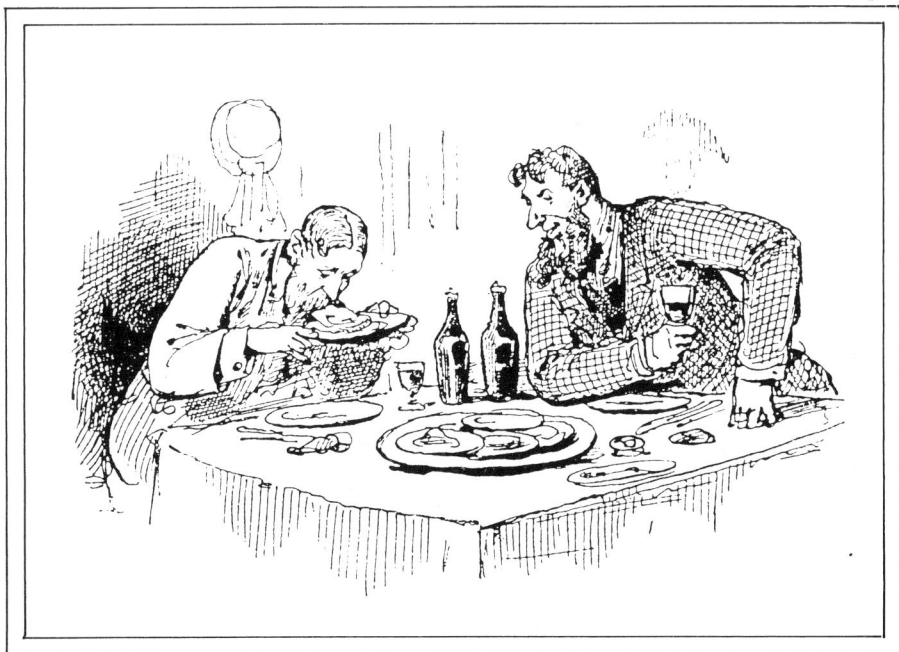

GIOVANNI'S

	49 – 55 Canterbury Road, Whitstable. Tel: (0227) 273034.
Hours:	*Open for lunch and dinner. Closed Monday.*
Average prices:	*A la carte from £18; lunch £8.95, dinner £11.*
Wines:	*House wine £6.25 per bottle.*

This lovely restaurant celebrated its 21st anniversary in June of 1989. Twenty-one years of quiet success as Whitstable's favourite restaurant, esteemed and highly regarded throughout the length and breadth of the county and with a reputation of truly international standing. This has been achieved through the care and devotion of the Ferrari family, whose attention to detail extends throughout the restaurant, from the careful selection of the very best Scottish wild salmon, to the Aberdeen Angus beef, the Kentish lamb, the finest game and the freshest and best seafood and fish available. Starters from the imaginative menu include real turtle soup with sherry, cream of asparagus, minestrone and chicken broth with egg parsley and parmesan cheese as well as many others. Crabs, lobsters, fresh fish, Scottish beef and English roasts are featured as well as one of the finest Italian menus to be found in the south-east, as might well be expected, with a mouth-watering selection of classical and regional Italian specialities, prepared and cooked to perfection. Desserts are also exceptional, and the unobtrusive yet attentive service is an added delight.

Italian and French Cuisine.   Whitstable, Kent. Tel: (0227) 273034

MARCHESI

	Albion Street, Broadstairs. Tel: (0843) 62481.
Hours:	*Open for lunch and dinner every day.*
Average prices:	*A la carte £15 to £20; table d'hôte lunch £10.*
Wines:	*£5.75 per bottle.*

Recognition by all the major food guides has done nothing to spoil this superb restaurant. Marchesi was there long before Egon Ronay was born, and is probably the reason that food guides started being published — to select restaurants of true excellence from the many that give poor value for money. This restaurant has been in the hands of one family for over 104 years, and owners the Roger family, who also own and run Broadstairs' famed Royal Albion Hotel, know that there is never any substitute for quality in every aspect of running a restaurant. Quality is apparent from the moment you enter and enjoy the delightful decor, the warmth of welcome and the impressive choice of wines on display in the wine racks. The menus give huge choice, and since everything is fresh each day (apart from well hung meat and properly seasoned game) you are certain of the very best. The fishermen bring their catch here each day, as they have done for generations, and it is small wonder that this, the oldest established restaurant in Kent, is also the most esteemed and popular in the county. Booking is essential — for their 'French nights' you will need to book weeks in advance. All cards.

MARCHESI

Albion Street, Broadstairs, Kent. Tel: (0843) 62481

THE ROYAL ALBION HOTEL

Albion Street
Broadstairs
Call us FREE on 0800 521130
Telex No. 0843 965761

THE ROYAL ALBION HOTEL

Albion Street, Broadstairs.
Tel: (0800) 521130. Telex: (0843) 965761.

Hours:	*Full hotel hours. Open for lunch and dinner every day.*
Average prices:	*A la carte from £15.50.*
Wines:	*From £5.75 per bottle.*

Broadstairs' famed Royal Albion Hotel is part of the history of this lovely and historic town. It was here that Charles Dickens wrote much of Nicholas Nickleby, and the hotel owns the original letter that Dickens wrote to a close friend, praising both Broadstairs and the hotel. The hotel has been modernised to the highest standards, has 20 splendidly appointed bedrooms, all with every amenity including direct dial telephones, colour televisions with remote control, tea/coffee making equipment, clock-radio alarms and in-house video programmes. The views over Broadstairs harbour and bay are truly breathtaking, and many of the rooms have balconies and steps which lead right down to the lawns and gardens, the promenade and the beach!

There is always a lot going on at the Royal Albion; there are trips to France organised, golfing weekends, and special gourmet evenings and events. Peter Roger, director of the hotel, is very much a wine expert, a Chevalier of the Order of St. Vincent de Flandres, and throughout the year he organises special wine events which are attended by enthusiasts, and addressed by wine experts from both sides of the channel. The hotel, and the famed Marchesi restaurant, are both owned and run by the Roger family, and the three sons, David, John and Peter Roger are actively engaged in every aspect of the business. Guests can dine in the hotel itself or at Marchesi (see separate entry), the oldest restaurant in the county, and probably the oldest in the country to have been in the hands of one family for over 104 years!

In addition, the hotel is the ideal venue for the businessman, whether for a directors' lunch or dinner, or to take advantage of the excellent conference facilities offered by the hotel. There is a 100 seater functions room, a private boardroom for meetings of up to ten people, and all amenities from flip charts and videos to translation and secretarial services. There is a private car park, and a courtesy bus is run by the hotel with Kent International Airport less than ten minutes drive away. Preferential business rates can be negotiated and special banquetting menus discussed and arranged.

The first rate facilities lend themselves just as easily to weddings and other social gatherings, and there are special 'Champagne Weekends' for those seeking a romantic break, where luxury accommodation is complemented by such extravagant touches as Belgian chocolates in the room, a full English breakfast-in-bed and a bottle of champagne each evening with dinner. A splendid hotel and legendary restaurant. All leading credit cards welcome.

THE CROWN INN

The Street, Finglesham, Deal. Tel: (0304) 612555.

Hours: *Open for morning coffee, lunch and dinner every day.*
Average prices: *Bar meals from £1.95 to £3.95; a la carte dinner £10.*
Wines: *From £5.50 per bottle.*

'Where to Eat — Kent' discovered this most delightful country inn as a direct result of repeated recommendations from readers of the guide. There is no better accolade, and it is good to see such a successful inn set in an off-the-beaten-track location. To find The Crown, take the A258 Deal to Sandwich road; the village of Finglesham is midway between the two, a half mile off the A258; signposted. Here are real ales, Shepherd Neame Masterbrew, Ruddles County and Websters Yorkshire; good sound home-cooking and a fine atmosphere in which to enjoy same. Old flagstones, inglenook open log fires, a fine garden and good food. There is a daily special on the blackboard — several in fact — with steak & kidney pie, paprika beef, fillet of cod creole style, cinzano kidney and others. Three course Sunday lunch is just £6.25 and table d'hôte dinner £6.95 on Friday nights only. The à la carte has plenty to choose from with starters of whitebait, pâté and toast, prawn cocktail and mussels in garlic. The main courses include a delectable chicken Napoleon, which is supreme of chicken, pan fried in butter with cognac and orange sauce, bacon, onions and mushrooms. Lots of choice; great steaks; fresh fish. Access, Visa. Try the Friday night three course special at £6.95!

THE CROWN INN
The Street, Finglesham, Deal.
Tel: (0304) 612555

WARD'S RESTAURANT & HOTEL

Earl's Avenue, Folkestone, Kent. Tel: (0303) 45166.

Hours: *Full hotel hours. Open every day for coffee, lunch and dinner.*
Average prices: *A la carte from £16.50; lunch £8.95; Sun lunch £9.95.*
Wines: *House wine from £6.25 to £23 per bottle.*

It would be hard to find a more elegant and sophisticated hotel anywhere near Folkestone. Ward's has become a great favourite, offering ten sumptuous bedroom suites, each designed to the highest standards with stylish *en suite* bathrooms, direct dial phones, colour televisions and tea/coffee making facilities. Restaurateurs for more than 17 years, Ron and Pat Ward have combined their skills with those of brother Roger and son Andrew to create a haven of excellence which pervades the entire establishment. Three of the fine bedrooms even have fitted whirlpools, and the hotel has live jazz every Thursday evening, and appropriate theme music on other special gourmet evenings. Menus change every few days, and such is the variety and scope of choice that little more than an impression may be given in the space available. A la carte has several starters, from home-made soup to Norwegian prawn salad; warm chicken livers with crispy bacon to moules marinière. Main course selections number about eight to twelve, depending on fresh seasonal availability, and include all the great favourites, with fish and seafood, steaks and charcoal grilled specialities plus many more. Lovely and original desserts, and a selection of around 40 wines. All major cards.

WARD'S RESTAURANT & HOTEL
Earl's Avenue, Folkestone.
Telephone: 0303 45166

THE HYTHE IMPERIAL HOTEL

Hythe. Tel: (0303) 267441.
Hours: *Open for coffee, lunch and dinner (last orders 9pm).*
Average prices: *Table d'hôte £13.50; Sun lunch £12.50.*
Wines: *House wine £7.50 per bottle.*

The imposing Hythe Imperial stands in its own idyllic 52 acre estate on the seafront, and offers a golf course, croquet lawn, grass and hard tennis courts, bowls and putting as well as lovely gardens. An ideal venue for conferences, weddings and functions of all descriptions, the Victorian hotel exudes a feeling of luxury and comfort as soon as guests enter the panelled foyer, resplendent with its traditional leather seating. The Prince's Room Restaurant, which has been completely restyled, is particularly lovely. The menu is international in concept; starters include lasagne, salade de crevettes, coupe esteval or soupe de volaille. Main courses offer grilled trout 'Cleopatre', roast Kentish turkey with all the trimmings, veal cooked in lemon butter with pistachio nuts and toasted pine kernels, pork fillet with onions and celery in cream and brandy, or prime Scottish steak — New York style. A fine wine list with some notable Bordeaux accompanies.

THE ABBOT'S FIRESIDE

High Street, Elham. Tel: (0303) 84265.

Hours:	*Open for dinner Tues, Wed, Thurs, Fri and Sat evenings.*
Average prices:	*A la carte menu at set price; lunch or dinner £12.50; Sun lunch £6.95.*
Wines:	*From £6.50 per bottle.*

Not only is The Abbot's Fireside a fine restaurant, it is also one of the best examples of pre-renaissance architecture in the country and is thought to have been built around 1400 from mediaeval design. Elaborate carved decorations of the 13th to 14th century grace the building, and the carved beam above the spit-roasting fireplace was pillaged from the archbishop's palace at Lyminge. Your hosts are owners Richard, Robert and Irene Napper who greet your arrival. Formerly chef at some of the finest hotels and restaurants, Robert has practised his art at Claridges — which he chose instead of accepting a position at Buckingham Palace — culminating in his becoming a lecturer in advanced catering, and adviser to the United Nations. Richard is the wine expert, with distinguished qualifications and experience — including that of the art of spit-roasting. The spit-roast operates on Wed & Fri evenings only. Roasts vary from whole pig to pheasants, lamb, ducks, guinea fowl and even partridges. Prices include service and VAT. It should be borne in mind that booking is essential at weekends; advisable at other times.

The Abbot's Fireside

High Street, Elham. Tel: (0303) 84265

THE BLACK HORSE

Fiddling Lane, Monk's Horton, Sellindge, Nr. Ashford. Tel: (0303) 812182.

Hours: *Open every day of the week for lunch and dinner except Mon and Sun eve. (last orders 10pm).*

Average prices: *A la carte £8; Sun lunch £4.95 (main course); bar snacks from £1 to £10.*

Wines: *From £5 per bottle.*

When many country inns are feeling the pinch, it is a very special pleasure to discover such an inn as The Black Horse. Here is an inn which is thriving with activity, life and fine food and wine. Pat and Ray Cottingham have built up a most enviable reputation, and their inn is as pretty as a picture. Set amid pastures and woodland, the barbecue is famous — not only for excellence, but also because it can operate in all weathers. There are real ales — five to choose from — and there is live music every Sunday evening. The menu is a delight, and is one of the most comprehensive you are likely to find anywhere in Kent. A whole selection of appetising starters precede home-made dishes ranging from sweet and sour pork to fresh salmon and prawn gratin; from a variety of pizzas to beef bourguignon. There are sirloin, rump and fillet steak; a fresh fish selection, as well as some specialities of the house plus salads. Snacks include filled jacket potatoes, sandwiches and many more.

The Black Horse
Fiddling Lane, Monk's Horton, Sellindge, Nr. Ashford, Kent.
Tel: (0303) 812182.

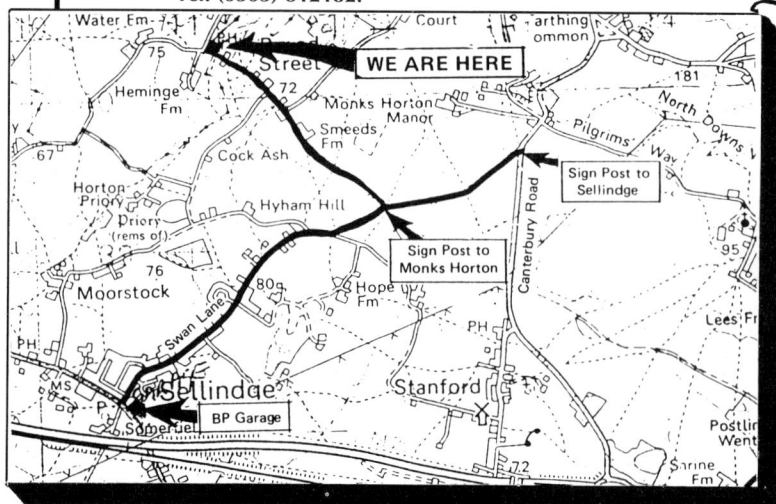

THE SHIP HOTEL

High Street, New Romney. Tel: (0679) 62776.

Hours: *Open for morning coffee, lunch and dinner (last orders 10pm). Closed for food on Sunday evenings.*

Average prices: *A la carte £10; Sun lunch £6.50; snacks from £2.*

Wines: *From £5 per bottle.*

Michael and Pamela Little run a tight ship. Only 'tight' of course in the sense that they are most sober and serious in the selection of the very best for their excellent menus, choosing the best catch from the day's selection from the nearby fishing boats, and fruit, vegetables, meat and poultry from local suppliers. The Ship Hotel is a genuine unspoilt English inn with eight fine bedrooms, modernised to today's standards at prices which are considered to be more than just reasonable. Ideally located for exploring the legendary Romney Marshes, this is the idyllic setting from which to explore the fine old churches, bird sanctuaries and numerous other attractions of the region. Fine beaches at nearby Littlestone and Greatstone; fresh and salt-water fishing; deep sea fishing too. You can even take flying lessons at nearby Lydd Flying Schools where the South-East College of Air Training has its base. The Ship Hotel offers the very best of inn-style home-cooking, and the ever-changing menu offers Kentish lamb, Dover sole, whole plaice off the bone, lemon sole, cod and other fish in season. Access/Visa welcome.

THE SHIP HOTEL

HIGH STREET, NEW ROMNEY. TEL: (0679) 62776

THE FLACKLEY ASH HOTEL AND RESTAURANT

	Peasmarsh, near Rye. Tel: (079 721) 651.
Hours:	*Open for lunch, dinner and bar meals.*
Average prices:	*A la carte £12–17; lunch £9.50.*
Wines:	*House wine £7 per bottle.*

Situated just over the border in Sussex, a few miles from the Cinque Port town of Rye, The Flackley Ash is a true country house hotel, offering not only high standards of comfort and cuisine but also a fine leisure club, which includes a solarium, swimming pool, sauna and more. There are, in total, 30 bedrooms, all *en suite* and appointed to high standards, and banqueting facilities for up to 100 guests. The restaurant has earned itself a splendid reputation, with fresh fish being very much a speciality of the house. The *fruits de mer* platter is always an attraction and there is an extensive, but not expensive à la carte selection from which you may choose meat, game and poultry dishes, or, perhaps, the Flackley Ash carpetbagger steak with oysters and mushrooms, or veal in a ginger wine sauce. A choice of six house wines comprises part of the list, and, for those seeking a lighter bite, bar meals are available too. All major cards are welcome. Hosts are Clive and Jeanie Bennett.

THE PINK ELEPHANT REAL ALE AND WINE BAR

	High Street, Tenterden. Tel: (05806) 4972.
Hours:	*Open for coffee, lunch and dinner.*
Average prices:	*A la carte £2.50 to £10.*

Phil Ubee and Peter Howitt (Joey from the TV series 'Bread') own and run this excellent and fun wine bar. Straight out of the Great Gatsby era, the Pink Elephant is full of character and good food. Prawns in the shell with garlic dip, kebabs, Italian dishes and Greek specialities are some of the varied and interesting treats in store. Real ales, of course, and a fine selection of wines to choose from — all at reasonable prices. Great fun. You will find the Pink Elephant opposite Boots the Chemist.

THE WILLIAM CAXTON

West Cross, High Street, Tenterden. Tel: (05806) 3142.

Hours: *Open for coffee, lunch and dinner (last orders 9pm).*
                         Restaurant closed Sun and Wed evening. Bar meals daily.

Average prices: *Snacks from £1.25; bar meals from about £4.50.*

Wines: *House wine £5.25 per bottle; £1 per glass.*

This delightful traditional-style country inn, with its old beams, open log fires and friendly atmosphere is certainly one of the most popular in the whole of the area. Terry and Heather take great pride in the quality of the food and in every aspect of the running of this fine inn, and offer comfortable accommodation, with a full English breakfast, at remarkably reasonable prices. The breakfast has become almost a legend, with fruit juices, cereals, sausage, bacon, egg, tomatoes and mushrooms, kippers, haddock, crisp toast and marmalade and freshly brewed coffee. Later in the day there are real ales at the bar (Wethereds Winter Royal, Fremlins and Flowers) and plenty of fine home-cooked dishes to choose from. Rump steaks are a speciality, but there are daily specials both at lunchtime and in the evening, and a goodly variety of other home-made dishes to choose from. Salads, pies, casseroles and seafood are always popular, and the crisply battered cod is a dish that attracts folk from miles around. Good sound home-cooked food in an unspoilt and delightful inn.

THE WILLIAM CAXTON
West Cross, High Street, Tenterden.
Telephone: (05806) 3142

THE WHITE LION HOTEL

	High Street, Tenterden. Tel: (05806) 2921. Fax: 05806 4157.
Hours:	*Open for coffee, lunch, tea and dinner. Bar meals.*
Average prices:	*A la carte from £15; table d'hôte £10 (lunch), £11 (dinner); snacks from £1.10.*
Wines:	*House wine £6.25 per bottle.*

This lovely old historic coaching inn hotel is now one of the progressive Resort Hotels establishments. Spacious and gracious, it is Tenterden's premier hotel, and though not large (there are some 14 bedrooms at present) it is currently undergoing a complete refurbishment programme which will include new modern kitchens to match the brilliant reputation for good food which has been one of the most appreciated changes under the new owners. All rooms have colour televisions, direct dial telephones and tea/coffee making equipment and the hotel also offers fine conference facilities in two suites, the main one being for up to 30 delegates, and the secondary for smaller gatherings such as directors' meetings. The restaurant seats 60, and menus change constantly to take advantage of seasonal specialities, game, fresh fish, vegetables and fruit. The style is traditionally English, with roasts, casseroles, salads and fresh fish from Rye Bay as well as game, poultry and other seasonal specialities. The lunch menu is one of the best in town, with a daily blackboard menu in the main bar. The refurbishment will be completed by April 1990, adding more bedrooms and a new 50 seater conference suite to existing facilities. All major cards welcome.

THE WHITE LION

HIGH STREET, TENTERDEN, KENT. (058 06) 2921

THE CROWN

Stone-in-Oxney, Tenterden, Kent. Tel: (023 383) 267.

Hours: *Open for lunch and dinner (last orders 9.30pm).*

Average prices: *From £1 to £8.*

Wines: *From £5 per bottle.*

Just along the quiet country lanes from Wittersham, you will find this small country inn. Here are real log fires, a shady garden, traditional ales and good home-cooked food. Unspoilt, and in one of the loveliest parts of the county, The Crown inn is well known not only for the good home-cooking but also for the fine live-music evenings that have long been a feature of the inn. These vary according to availability of the musicians so that it is wise to call in advance to find 'What's on' — and that includes the menu as there is no food on music nights, they're far too busy! There is an outdoor barbecue in summer, set on an attractive patio and with tables and benches in the garden and summer umbrellas. There is an ample car park too and the inn is less than twenty minutes away from the ancient cinque port of Rye. The Romney Marshes are adjoining Stone-in-Oxney, and there are some beautiful river walks (and fine fishing too) all around the area. Everything is available in the way of snacks, including sandwiches, ploughman's and salads. No credit cards.

THE CROWN
Stone-in-Oxney, Tenterden, Kent. Tel: (023 383) 267

61

YE MAYDES RESTAURANT

High Street, Biddenden. Tel: (0580) 291306.

Hours: *Open for lunch and dinner (last orders 9.30 pm). Closed Sun/ Mon.*

Average prices: *A la carte £15; lunch £9.50 (set price).*

Wines: *From £6 per bottle.*

One of the best known restaurants in the county, Ye Maydes is also one of the longest established and most popular. Sheila Daniels, the owner of Ye Maydes, has built up a fabulous reputation for the restaurant, and it is her stringent insistence that only the very very best will do, that has earned her accolades galore. The menu is a happy combination of English and French selections. Fillet of trout with champagne, roast duckling with a walnut and cherry sauce and lamb kidneys forestière are some of the examples from a menu which changes every month, using fresh fish, game in season, unusual recipes and old favourites. There is a very strong 'following' of regular customers, not surprisingly, and it is most advisable to book in advance. This lovely ancient cottage building was once used by the Flemish weavers; it is intimate, cosy, warm and quaint, with great open fires and polished oak furniture, set in the old village of Biddenden. Access, Visa and American Express cards welcome.

THE BELL

Smarden. Tel: (023 377) 283.

Hours:	*Open for lunch and dinner*
Average prices:	*A la carte £1.10 to £8.25.*
Wines:	*House wine £4.95 per bottle; £1 per glass.*

'The minute you walk in the place you know that this is the real thing! The floor is made of huge ancient flagstones; the massive oak beams, great logs in the cavernous inglenook fireplaces and genuine antique furniture will make you feel that you have stepped backward in time. Built in 1536, The Bell became an inn in 1769, and has for many many years enjoyed a reputation for fine food second to none. Small wonder that this inn was chosen to be featured in the American magazine *Newsweek*. Spacious gardens with flowering shrubs, trees and flower borders, set in the very heart of the garden of England, with tables and benches to enjoy your meal and drinks al fresco if you wish. Good home-cooked food ranges from simple sandwiches and ploughman's lunches to home-baked ham and gammon steaks, Cumberland pie, fillet and rump steaks, chilli con carne, steak and kidney pie and lasagne, to name but a few from a wide selection. Crunch cake, bread pudding and apple crumble are some of the desserts featured on the menu. There is a children's room, and lovely accommodation is available with four double rooms, but DO book well in advance to avoid disappointment. Access and Visa (Mastercard) welcome.

Smarden (023 377) 283

THE KING'S ARMS

High Street, Headcorn. Tel: (0622) 890216.

Hours:	*Open for lunch and dinner (last orders 10pm).*
Average prices:	*A la carte £10; snacks from £1.*
Wines:	*House wine £5.35 per bottle.*

Where to Eat — Kent is again delighted to feature this fine English country inn, The King's Arms. It is hoped that we have contributed to the great success of this inn, which has led to its having had almost to double the size of the restaurant — by public demand! The reason, of course, is the lovely home-cooked food for which the inn is renowned. Fresh fish every day with fresh dressed crab, shell-on prawns in garlic, salmon steaks, plaice and cod. A house speciality is the grilled fresh sardine dish, and the home baked gammon is another you should try. At £6.50, the roast Sunday lunches are exceptional value and it is wise to book in advance. The menu varies from day to day, but you are almost always certain of the superb fillet of beef Stroganoff, the fresh plaice with cheese sauce, and the steak and kidney pie. There is live entertainment in the bar almost every week, and the inn has a nice garden, with outdoor barbecues in summer. The inn dates from the 18th century, and offers comfortable accommodation. Ideally placed for trips to Leeds Castle, the Pilgrim's Way, Headcorn aerodrome, home of the London Flight Centre and parachute club. Why not drop in?

THE KINGS ARMS
HEADCORN

THE BELL INN

High Street, Staplehurst. Tel: (0580) 891322.

Hours:	*Open for morning coffee, lunch and dinner. The restaurant proper is open from Wed to Sat inclusive for dinner.*
Average prices:	*Lunch from £2 to £4.50; dinner £5 to £8.*
Wines:	*From £5.75 per bottle.*

David and Margaret Monks are now the proprietors of this comfortable inn, and they have completely refurbished it. A most welcoming establishment, The Bell Inn has four fine letting rooms including a family room, and all are priced remarkably competitively at £20 per person per night. This price includes a full English breakfast in the finest traditions of the word, with cereal, toast, home-made bread, fresh coffee and bacon, sausages, mushrooms and tomatoes freshly cooked to order. In fact, traditional English fare is the theme of The Bell, and the home-made pies include a speciality not to be found elsewhere — Bell Pie. This is made from a secret recipe which creates a delicious sausage meat, cheese and apple pie of great popularity! There is steak & kidney pie of course, plus fisherman's pie, crofter's pie and a fine steak and Guinness casserole too. Excellent steaks including rump and sirloin, and a trencherman's mixed grill. You might also sample snacks such as ploughman's, salads and filled baps, plus a full range of delicious desserts. The Bell is proud of the lunchtime specials which change each day, and the inn has facilities for private parties and functions. Open log fires; large car park.

The Bell Inn

HIGH STREET, STAPLEHURST. (0580) 891322

Kennel Holt
COUNTRY HOUSE HOTEL

KENNEL HOLT HOTEL, CRANBROOK, KENT, TN17 2PT.
TELEPHONE: (0580) 712032   FACSIMILE: (0580) 712931

THE KENNEL HOLT COUNTRY HOUSE HOTEL

Cranbrook. Tel: (0580) 712032. Fax: (0580) 712931.

Hours:	*Open for lunch, tea, dinner (last orders 9pm) and Sun lunch. Closed Sun evenings except for residents.*
Average prices:	*Dinner £19.75; lunch (3 course) £11.50; Sun lunch £16.75.*
Wines:	*House wine £7.45 per bottle. Fine selection.*

The Kennel Holt Hotel is now regarded as one of the finest country house hotels in the county, and the reputation for excellence and value for money has contributed to the great popularity which it now enjoys. David and Jane Misseldine have taken the fullest possible advantage of the rural setting of this exquisite country house, and it is here that peace and tranquillity take on a new meaning. Located on the main road between Goudhurst and Cranbrook, you will have to keep an eye open for the hotel's sign at the roadside, for The Kennel Holt is to be found, set in landscaped gardens, down a private drive, well away from the sounds of traffic. The house itself is Elizabethan, and is both elegant and graceful, yet there is an informality that will put you at your ease the moment you arrive. This is the ideal place at which to stay if you are visiting the area, as you are well located to visit Scotney Castle, Bodiam, Leeds Castle, Headcorn Aerodrome (with its famous parachute club and London Flight Centre training school) — whilst Sissinghurst Castle is within walking distance.

The restaurant seats 32, and on Friday and Saturday evenings there is usually a pianist to create the right atmosphere in which to enjoy the fine food. Guests are welcomed first with drinks (waiter-served in crystal) in one of the two fine lounges, before moving on to the dining room. However, because of the way in which the menu changes, literally from day to day, it is most difficult to do more than give an impression of the variety which will seduce you! The great British traditional dishes feature large on all menus with the famed roast beef of Olde England, Yorkshire pudding and fresh vegetables, properly hung game in season, poultry, fresh fish, seafood and Kentish lamb.

There is a wide choice of the daily luncheon menu, and chefs Ian Best and Peter Miller give every bit as much attention to this as to the dinner menu. You may choose between the three course lunch at £11.50 or a full five course spread at £18.75.

The quality of the wine cellar is well known, with English wines from Lamberhurst, Penshurst and Chiddingstone featuring strongly, and a selection of fine Burgundies also prominent. Particular attention is given to the choice of house wines; they are not the cheapest wines, for they are chosen for quality not price, and the house claret is especially good. The Kennel Holt is open for lunch every day; booking in advance is always advisable.

The ten bedrooms are all *en suite*, with all facilities such as direct dial telephone, colour television etc. All leading credit cards are accepted.

THE ROYAL OAK

	Iden Green, Benenden. Tel: (0580) 240585.
Hours:	*Open for lunch and dinner (last orders 9.45pm).*
Average prices:	*A la carte £6–£12; Sun lunch £7.50; snacks from £2.*
Wines:	*From £5.95 per bottle. Halves available.*

This truly excellent inn has something of the feel of the 'British Raj' about it. Bentwood furniture, punkah fans and filigree gold wrought iron are something completely different. David and Rita Drewett, owners of The Royal Oak, have won just about every award and accolade imaginable including 'Best Pub in the South East' (twice), the Dutch Dairy Board's cookery prize (again twice) and many others. This is a super inn and you will not find a better cold cabinet in the county. Seafood, salads, poultry, roasts, game, shellfish, crabs and lobsters, smoked fish, quiches and cheeses as well as pulses and at least 25 choices of sweets! Sunday lunch is always most popular — do book in advance — for you may choose from a light snack to a full two, three, four or even five course meal. There is a special children's menu, and the à la carte in the evenings compares with many of the noted restaurants in the county. Dave and Rita also own The Star Inn in nearby Rolvenden where the food is of similar quality. Excellent daily specials range in price from £2.50 to £7.35 and include such dishes as fresh sole with new potatoes and peas, Bishop's Beef (beef in red wine with stilton & cream) and others. All major cards.

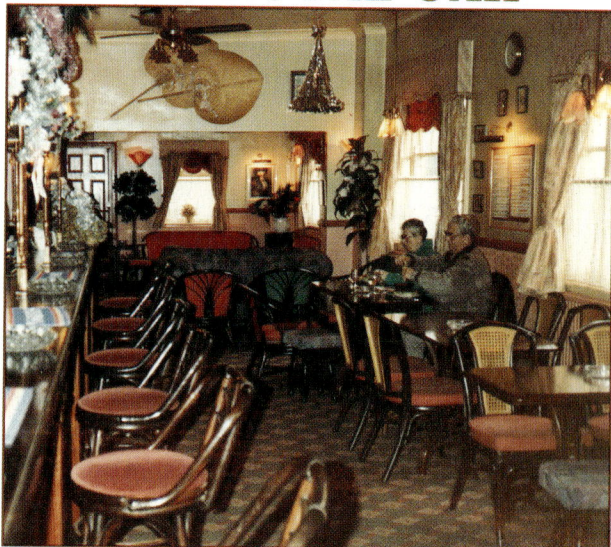

THE ROYAL OAK

IDEN GREEN BENENDEN. Tel: (0580) 240585

THE BULL INN

The Street, Sissinghurst. Tel: (0580) 712821.

Hours: *Restaurant open for dinner Tues – Sat (Last orders 10pm). Bar meals served every day, lunch and dinner. Open 11am to 11pm.*

Average prices: *Bar meals from £1.50; dinner £12 (2 course), £14 (3 course); Sun lunch £7.50.*

Wines: *From £5.75 to £20 per bottle.*

The Bull Inn dates from the 13th century, and was featured in the book 'The Broad Highway' as the perfect example of a true village inn. But far more than just this, here is an inn renowned for its fine food throughout the county. Fresh whole crabs and lobsters feature most of the time on the excellent menus alongside locally caught rainbow trout, prime roast beef, Kentish lamb, honey-roast ham, turbot with shellfish sauce, monkfish in oyster sauce, pheasant in port wine and some of the most succulent steaks you will see in Kent! There are daily specials featured on the blackboard, and the bar menu offers sandwiches, ploughman's lunches, salads, toasted sandwiches and other delights and delectations. First class accommodation too, in beautifully modernised, luxurious, fully *en suite* bedrooms (double and twin rooms) all with colour televisions. A really genuine English inn with real ales, a lovely garden, private car park and a 32 seat restaurant.

THE BULL INN
The Street, Sissinghurst. Telephone: (0580) 712821

THE QUEEN'S HEAD HOTEL

Rye Road, Hawkhurst. Tel: (0580) 753577.

Hours: *Open for morning coffee, lunch and dinner (last orders 10pm). Closed Sun night and Monday.*

Average prices: *A la carte £18; Sun lunch £9.95; bar meals from £4 to £8.50.*

Wines: *From £6.50 per bottle; £1.10 per glass.*

The ancient and very lovely Queen's Head Hotel is really a part of the history of this town. An architectural delight, it is as attractive inside as out, with massive oak beams, huge fireplaces, fine accommodation and spacious elegant functions facilities. The hotel has eight double bedrooms and one single, all *en suite* and with every comfort (T.V., tea/coffee equipment, mini-bar, trouser press, telephone etc) and, under new owners, has been substantially re-appointed to very high standards. Accommodating up to 150 guests, this is ideal for weddings too — in fact all types of private function can be fully catered for. The 30 seater restaurant features both French and English fare and with dishes like the prawns from the Indian ocean in white wine, glazed with cheese, bacon, soya and garlic as just one of an imaginative range of starters — followed by local pheasant, roasted in its own marinade, or a fabulous entrecote Café de Paris in a herbal butter with no less than fifteen ingredients, it is small wonder that you need to book. All major cards.

THE QUEEN'S HEAD HOTEL   Rye Road, Hawkhurst, Kent.
Tel: (0580) 753577

THE ELEPHANT'S HEAD

Hook Green, Lamberhurst. Tel: (0892) 890279.

Hours: *Open for coffee, lunch and dinner.*

Average prices: *A la carte from £4; snacks from £1.*

Wines: *From under £5.*

In the heart of the countryside, midway between Tunbridge Wells and the village of Lamberhurst, is one of the loveliest settings in the county, The Elephant's Head restaurant, which is 500 years old and complete with beamed ceilings and blazing log fires, seats 28 and the evening menu specialises in top quality local produce, House specials include steaks, or you could try the roast duckling, salmon steaks, trout, chicken and scampi, The chef's special is extremely popular and the inn has a good salad bar, the lunch menu features many old favourites, all home-cooked, including steak and kidney pie made with real ale. Home-made soups are offered on both the lunch and evening menu. A full range of Harveys real ales, vintage ports and reasonably priced wine is complemented by attractive gardens, including a childrens play area. There are two large car parks.

THE ELEPHANT'S HEAD

HOOK GREEN, LAMBERHURST, KENT. Tel: (0892) 890279

71

THE SWAN INN

Lamberhurst Down, Lamberhurst. Tel: (0892) 890200.
Hours: *Open for lunch and dinner every day (last orders 10pm).*
Average prices: *From £2.50 to £8.50.*
Wines: *House wine £5.75 per bottle.*

One of the most charming and unspoilt inns in the whole of this part of the county, The Swan Inn at Lamberhurst is as pretty as a picture. The inn is next to the famed Lamberhurst vineyards and is set in the heart of the Weald of Kent with Scotney Castle a few hundred yards away, Bayham Abbey and lovely Bewl water within walking distance. Here is home-cooking at its very best, featuring local fruit and vegetables, grown in the garden of England, locally caught trout, game (in season) and fresh salads. There are daily specials on the blackboard, and the lunch menu features fresh fish — try the excellent seafood Mornay — pork in leek and stilton sauce and other delightful, delicious and original dishes. The Swan mixed grill enjoys well-deserved fame with Barnsley chop, gammon steak, rump steak, sausage, kidney, mushrooms and tomatoes: surely a challenge to any trencherman! A fine beer garden to enjoy in the summer, a haven of warmth and welcome inside in autumn and winter. Your hosts are John and Tammy Johnson.

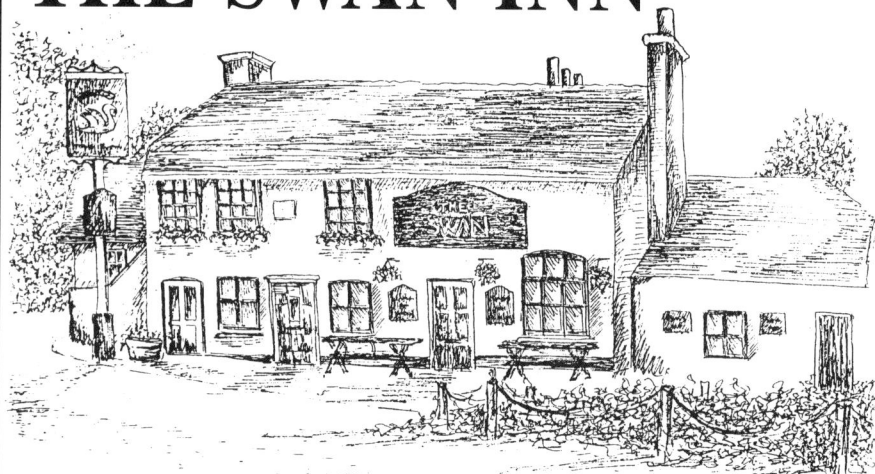

THE SWAN INN

LAMBERHURST DOWN, LAMBERHURST. Tel: (0892) 890200

THE GUN & SPITROAST INN

Goudhurst Road, Horsmonden. Tel: Brenchley 2925.

Hours:	*Open for morning coffee, lunch and dinner every day.*
Average prices:	*A la carte £15; Sun lunch £9.50; bar meals from £1.50–£5.*
Wines:	*House wine £7.60 per litre; selection to £65.*

Long known for its excellent food and famed spitroast, The Gun and Spitroast is now run by Lesley and David Ratcliffe. This fine characterful inn, with its historic connections, now has one of the best restaurants in the entire county, and head chef Tony Adams has used his considerable talents to enormous advantage in the preparation of a most innovative and clever menu. The genuine ancient spitroast is, of course, outstanding, and has long been the feature of this inn, for there never has been — or will be — a better way of cooking roasts than on a spit, sealing the juices in and adding a flavour which is totally unique. Beef or pork are roasted every day, and, on Saturdays both, plus game and poultry on occasion. The à la carte is varied too, and you may select from lobster thermidor, lobster americaine, skate wings deep fried in butter , carpetbagger steaks (stuffed with oysters), local game including pheasant and partridge in season as well as other specialities — including wild boar from time to time! The two restaurants seat 54 and 40 respectively. The bar menu is also very good indeed with a selection of old favourites from toasted sandwiches and ploughman's lunches to steaks, steak kidney and oyster pie etc. All cards welcome.

THE GUN & SPITROAST INN Goudhurst Road, Horsmonden
Tel. Brenchley 2925

WEEKS OF GOUDHURST

High Street, Goudhurst. Tel: (0580) 211380.
Hours: *Open for coffee, lunch and tea.*
Average prices: *Snacks £1 – £5.*

Weeks is both a bakery and a café/restaurant. Over the years it has built up a substantial local following for its produce and its success has generated nine bakery shops throughout the Weald of Kent. There are now branches in Battle, Mayfield, Pembury, Heathfield, Wadhurst, Staplehurst and Yalding, and in Goudhurst and Tenterden there are restaurants as well. Weeks is reminiscent of the bakeries of old. Here you can buy real bread, still warm from the oven, along with a whole range of buns, gateaux, cream cakes, spongy confections, scones and biscuits. The restaurant is open all day from 9am, serving coffee, snacks, teas and lunches (including Sunday). There are soups and starters, cottage pie, lasagne, moussaka, chicken supreme, jacket potatoes with all kinds of fillings, salads, ploughman's lunches and daily specials too. The desserts speak for themselves and the choice is extensive and tempting. Prices are also very reasonable and the staff friendly. The man behind the business is Peter Smith whose attention to detail and quality is well-known.

WEEKS OF GOUDHURST; Tenterden Restaurant, Bakery and Pâtisserie

THE GREEN CROSS INN

Goudhurst. Tel: (0580) 211200.

Hours: *Full licensing hours plus supper licence.*

Hosts Ian and Frances welcome you to this charming country house hotel/
inn. Goudhurst has long been favoured as one of the loveliest villages in
Kent, and The Green Cross Inn is the ideal place to stay whilst exploring
the many delights of the area. Sissinghurst and Scotney Castles; Bateman/s,
Bodiam, Bewl Water — all are nearby. There are six fine centrally heated
bedrooms, all with full amenities (colour T.V. etc), a large car park, open
fires in winter, a delightful restaurant and attractive garden. Real ales on
tap, and the food is outstanding. Steaks are the speciality of the House; the
entire rump and fillet is bought, and the restaurant cuts and cooks to the
most exacting requirement. The lunchtime menu is particularly good — and
very reasonable indeed. Offering Italian, French and English cooking, the
menu changes regularly and features traditional roasts, various excellent
salads, home-made pies (try the turkey and ham pie), and dishes such as
lasagne bolognese or beef and vegetables in red wine.

THE ROSE & CROWN

High Street, Brenchley. Tel: (089 272) 2107.

Hours:	*Restaurant open for dinner every night except Mon.*
Average prices:	*Dinner £14.95; Sun lunch £6.95; lunches £2.50 to £6.*
Wines:	*From £5.50 to £30 per bottle.*

The first licence was granted 'for the sale of ales and cider, but not on the Sabbath' in 1745, and this lovely ancient inn has been looking after the needs of the traveller ever since. More than this, here is an inn that has built up an enviable reputation for food, and is now in the most capable and imaginative hands of owners Rowley Hill and Alison Jones, whose personal touch is evident in every aspect of the inn. 12 fine bedrooms, all *en suite* with colour televisions, direct dial telephones, some with four-poster beds and one with jacuzzi — an ideal honeymoon suite. The restaurant menu changes regularly, but examples of starters and main courses might be along the following lines. Seafood gratin — prawns, scallops and mussels in white wine and cheese sauce; baked avocado with prawns in a tomato sauce, warm smoked turkey and Waldorf salad — these are some of the starters from a current menu. Main courses — pheasant in red wine, shark steaks in a basil and cream sauce, sole fillets with grapes and walnuts, rump steak cognac — with a brandy, cream and mustard sauce, and veal marsala. Fine home-made desserts too. The inn is renowned for the super traditional English breakfasts. Gourmet evenings, theme nights, private parties, conferences — The Rose & Crown is ideal. Visa, Amex, Access, Diners Club.

The Rose & Crown Inn

Telephone: Brenchley 2107
(089 272)

HIGH STREET
BRENCHLEY
Nr. TUNBRIDGE, KENT
TN12 7NQ

WEST END TAVERN

	West End, Marden. Tel: (0622) 831956.
Hours:	*Open for lunch (except Sun) and dinner (last orders 10pm; Sun 9.30pm).*
Average prices:	*Snacks from 80p; a la carte £8 to £10.*
Wines:	*House wine £5 per bottle; others from £5 up.*

The West End Tavern is as good a reason to visit the pretty village of Marden as any you may think of. Fine food is no stranger to this part of the garden of England, for it is here that the annual Marden Fruit Show is held, attracting visitors from all over the world. What better place to lunch — or dine — than this fine inn, where home-cooking is the order of the day, everything fresh and cooked to order. Hughie and Sylvia Shaw run the inn, and their varying menu always include fresh fish, steaks, vegetarian dishes, and a whole range of house specials such as their very popular mixed grill, with steak, sausage, bacon, liver, mushrooms, peas, chips and tomatoes. Basket meals and salads, curries, chicken supreme and chicken Kiev, chilli con carne and kebabs are always available, as are sandwiches, ploughman's lunches, filled roll selections and lots of extras like jacket potatoes and fried onion rings. Lovely old traditional dishes such as pease pudding, boiled bacon and Lancashire hot-pot. Good choice of wine with French, German, Yugoslavian and other selections. real ales on draught include Harveys, Fremlins and guest ales.

WEST END TAVERN
West End, Marden (0622) 831956

THE WILD DUCK

	Marden Thorn, Marden, Kent. Tel: (0622) 831340.
Hours:	*Open for lunch and dinner every day except Sunday evening, and all day Monday when the restaurant is closed.*
Average prices:	*A la carte £12 to £15; bar snacks from £1.*
Wines:	*From £5.50 per bottle; £1.10 per glass.*

Now here is a little inn that really is away from the madding crowd. In the very heart of rural Kent, The Wild Duck is set amid meadows and orchards midway between Marden and Staplehurst, just a few miles from Goudhurst and Cranbrook and not too far from Maidstone. Very well worth the drive, you will feel that you have discovered an oasis of peace, tranquillity and good home-cooked food. The restaurant menu offers over eight starters including wild duck liver pâté, home-made soup, crispy fried whitebait, Scottish smoked salmon and Chinese spare ribs. Fish, poultry and game, steaks and grills are on the main course menu with fresh grilled trout, poached salmon, deep fried scampi and lemon sole fillets, roast wild duck, breast of chicken stuffed with asparagus, fresh local pheasant with walnut stuffing and red wine sauce plus a whole range of mixed grills, steaks, cutlets and roast meats. The sweet trolley follows — and 'never-ending' coffee too. Visa and Access welcome, and there is a delightful garden with tables and amusements for the children. Marquee available for weddings and parties. Real ales. Excellent bar meals, lovely atmosphere.

THE WILD DUCK

MARDEN THORN, MARDEN, KENT. Tel: (0622) 831340

WIN A GOURMET DINNER FOR TWO
AT A TOP LOCAL RESTAURANT
VOTE FOR THE

Where to Eat

RESTAURANT OF THE YEAR

We are looking for the Kent Restaurant of the Year, to be featured in the next edition of **Where to Eat.**

During the compilation of the next edition, we shall be asking the region's caterers for their choice of best eating place. However, we would like you, the readers — people who regularly dine out — to take part as well.

A form is provided below for you to tell us what you consider to be the best eating place in the area. It could be an establishment featured in this guide, or a recommendation of your own. And it doesn't matter whether you nominate a formal restaurant, a country inn, a town pub, a wine bar/bistro or even a coffee shop or tearoom.

In addition, the prize of a gourmet meal for two will be awarded to the reader who gives us the best reason for eating out rather than eating in (in not more than 20 words), irrespective of his/her choice of restaurant.

My choice for Restaurant of the Year is

_____

at _____

I prefer to eat out rather than eat in because

_____

_____

Name _____

Address _____

Please send your votes to:

Restaurant of the Year,
Where to Eat in Kent
Kingsclere Publications Ltd.,
2 Highfield Avenue,
Newbury, Berkshire, RG14 5DS

Glossary

To assist readers in making the sometimes confusing choice from the menu, we have listed some of the most popular dishes from restaurant featured in *Where to Eat* up and down the country, together with a brief, general explanation of each item. Of course, this can never be a comprehensive listing — regional trends result in variation in the preparation of each dish, and there's no accounting for the flair and versatility of the chef — but we hope it offers readers a useful guideline to those enigmatic menu items.

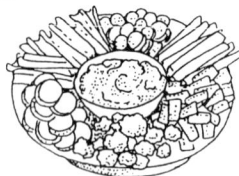

STARTERS

Foie gras .... duck or goose liver, often made into pâté
Gazpacho .... a chilled Spanish soup of onion, tomato, pepper and cucumber
Gravad lax .... raw salmon marinated in dill, pepper, salt and sugar
Guacamole .... a creamy paste of avocado flavoured with coriander and garlic
Hummus ..... a tangy paste of crushed chick peas flavoured with garlic and lemon
Meze .... a variety of spiced Greek hors d'oeuvre
Moules marinière .... mussels in a sauce of white wine and onions
Samosa .... small pastry parcels of spiced meat or vegetables
Satay ...... small skewers of grilled meat served with a spicy peanut dip
Taramasalata .... a creamy, pink paste of fish roe
Tzatziki .... yoghurt with cucumber and garlic
Vichyssoise .... a thick, creamy leek and potato soup, served cold

FISH

Bouillabaisse .... chunky fish stew from the south of France

Coquilles St Jacques .... scallops
Lobster Newburg .... with cream, stock and, sometimes, sherry
Lobster thermidor .... served in the shell with a cream and mustard sauce, glazed in the oven
Sole Walewska .... a rich dish of poached fish in a Mornay sauce with lobster
Sole bonne femme .... cooked with stock, dry white wine, parsley and butter
Sole véronique .... poached in a wine sauce with grapes
Trout meunière ...... floured, fried and topped with butter, parsley and lemon

MAIN COURSES

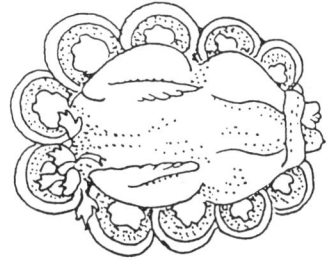

Beef Stroganoff .... strips of fillet steak sautéed and served in a sauce of wine and cream
Beef Wellington .... beef in a pastry crust
Boeuf Bourguignon ...... steak braised in a red wine sauce with onions, bacon and mushrooms
Chateaubriand .... thick slice of very tender fillet steak
Chicken à la King .... pieces of chicken in a creamy sauce
Chicken Kiev .... crumbed breast filled with herb butter, often garlic
Chicken Marengo .... with tomato, white wine and garlic
Chicken Maryland ...... fried and served with bacon, corn fritters and fried banana
Osso buco .... knuckle of veal cooked with white wine, tomato and onion
Pork Normandy .... with cider, cream and calvados
Ris de veau .... calves' sweetbreads
Saltimbocca alla romana ...... veal topped with ham, cooked with sage and white wine

Steak au poivre .... steak in a pepper and wine sauce
Steak bordelaise .... steak in red wine sauce with bone marrow
Steak Diane .... steak in a peppered, creamy sauce
Steak tartare .... raw, minced steak served with egg yolk
Tournedos Rossini ..... fillet steak on a croûton, topped with foie gras and truffles
Wiener Schnitzel .... escalope of veal, breadcrumbed and fried

SAUCES

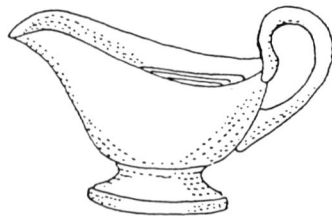

Aioli .... strong garlic mayonnaise
Anglaise .... thick white sauce of stock mixed with egg yolks, lemon and pepper
Arrabbiata .... tomatoes, garlic and hot peppers
Béarnaise .... thick sauce of egg yolks, vinegar, shallots, white wine and butter
Carbonara .... bacon, egg and Parmesan cheese
Chasseur .... mushrooms, tomatoes, shallots and white wine
Dijonnaise ...... cold sauce of eggs and mustard, similar to mayonnaise
Hollandaise .... egg yolks and clarified butter
Mornay ...... creamy sauce of milk and egg yolks flavoured with Gruyère cheese
Pesto .... basil, marjoram, parsley, garlic, oil and Parmesan cheese
Pizzaiola .... tomatoes, herbs, garlic and pepper
Provençale .... tomato, garlic, onion and white wine
Reform .... pepper and white wine with boiled egg whites, gherkins and mushrooms
Rémoulade .... mayonnaise with mustard, capers, gherkins and herbs, served cold

DESKERTS

Banoffi pie	with toffee and banana
Bavarois	cold custard with whipped cream and, usually, fruit
Crème brûlée	caramel-topped, rich vanilla flavoured cream
Crêpes Suzette	pancakes flavoured with orange or tangerine liqueur
Parfait	chilled dessert with fresh cream
Pavé	square shaped light sponge
Pavlova	meringue-based fruit dessert
Sabayon/zabaglione	whisked egg yolks, wine and sugar
Syllabub	whipped cream, wine and sherry
Zuccotto	a dome of liqueur-soaked sponge filled with fruit and cream
Zuppa inglese	an Italian trifle

CULINARY TERMS

Coulis	a thin purée of cooked vegetables or fruit
Croustade	a case of pastry, bread or baked potato which can be filled
Devilled	seasoned and spicy, often with mustard or cayenne
Dim-sum	various Chinese savoury pastries and dumplings
Duxelles	stuffing of chopped mushrooms and shallots
En croûte	in a pastry or bread case
Farce	a delicate stuffing
Feuilleté	filled slice of puff pastry
Florentine	containing spinach
Goujons	thin strips of fish
Julienne	cut into thin slices
Magret	a cut from the breast of a duck
Mille-feuille	thin layers of filled puff pastry
Quenelles	spiced fish or meat balls
Roulade	stuffed and rolled
Sauté	to brown in oil
Tournedos	small slice of thick fillet

Peckish in Perth?

Hungry in Holyhead?

Famished in Felixstowe?

Ravenous in Roscommon?

Where to Eat

The discerning diner's guide
to restaurants throughout
Britain and Ireland

*Copies available from bookshops
or direct from the publishers*
Kingsclere Publications Ltd
Use the Order Form overleaf

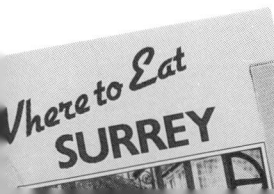

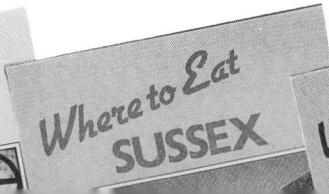

Where to Eat BERKSH

Where to Eat GLOUCESTERS & THE COTSW

Where to Eat CUMBRIA & THE LAKE DIST

Where to Eat NORTH EAS ENGLAND

Where to Eat YORKSHIRE & HUMBERSID

Where to Eat JERSEY

Where to Eat GUERNSEY

Where to Eat CORNWALL

Where to Eat SOMERSET

Where to Eat SURREY

Where to Eat SUSSEX

Where to Eat KENT

ORDER FORM

To:

KINGSCLERE PUBLICATIONS LTD.

Highfield House, 2 Highfield Avenue, Newbury, Berkshire, RG14 5DS

Please send me

____copies of *WHERE TO EAT in BERKSHIRE* @£1.95   £ _____

____copies of *WHERE TO EAT in BRISTOL, BATH & AVON* @£2.50   £ _____

____copies of *WHERE TO EAT in CHANNEL ISLANDS* @£1.50   £ _____

____copies of *WHERE TO EAT in CORNWALL* @£1.95   £ _____

____copies of *WHERE TO EAT in CUMBRIA & THE LAKE DISTRICT* @£1.95 £ _____

____copies of *WHERE TO EAT in DERBYS & THE PEAK DISTRICT* @£1.95 £ _____

____copies of *WHERE TO EAT in DORSET* @£2.50   £ _____

____copies of *WHERE TO EAT in EAST ANGLIA* @£2.95   £ _____

____copies of *WHERE TO EAT in EAST MIDLANDS* @£1.95   £ _____

____copies of *WHERE TO EAT in GLOS, OXON & THE COTSWOLDS* @£1.95 £ _____

____copies of *WHERE TO EAT in HAMPSHIRE* @£1.95   £ _____

____copies of *WHERE TO EAT in HERTS, BUCKS & BEDS* @£1.95   £ _____

____copies of *WHERE TO EAT in IRELAND* @£3.50   £ _____

____copies of *WHERE TO EAT in KENT* @£2.50   £ _____

____copies of *WHERE TO EAT in NORTH EAST ENGLAND* @£1.95   £ _____

____copies of *WHERE TO EAT in SCOTLAND* @£1.95   £ _____

____copies of *WHERE TO EAT in SOMERSET* @£1.95   £ _____

____copies of *WHERE TO EAT in SURREY* @£1.95   £ _____

____copies of *WHERE TO EAT in SUSSEX* @£2.95   £ _____

____copies of *WHERE TO EAT in WALES* @£3.50   £ _____

____copies of *WHERE TO EAT in WILTSHIRE* @£1.95   £ _____

____copies of *WHERE TO EAT in YORKS & HUMBERSIDE* @£1.95   £ _____

p&p at £0.50 (single copy), £1 (2 – 5 copies), £2 (6 copies)   £ _____

GRAND TOTAL £ _____

Name . . . .

Address . . . .

. . . .

Postcode . . . . Cheque enclosed for £ . . . .

Your help in answering the following would be appreciated:

(1) Did you buy this guide at a SHOP ☐   TOURIST OFFICE ☐   GARAGE ☐   OTHER ☐

(2) Are any of your favourite eating places *not* listed in this guide? If so, could you please supply names and locations . . . .

. . . .

. . . .

Index

ALPHABETICAL INDEX TO ESTABLISHMENTS

ALPHABETICAL INDEX TO TOWNS AND VILLAGES

i